Defoe and the Novel

Defoe and the Novel

EVERETT ZIMMERMAN

UNIVERSITY OF CALIFORNIA PRESS

Berkeley · Los Angeles · London

1975

University of California Press
Berkeley and Los Angeles, California
University of California Press, Ltd.
London, England
Copyright © 1975 by
The Regents of the University of California
ISBN: 0-520-02688-8
Library of Congress Catalog Card Number: 73-91682
Printed in the United States of America

Contents

Preface   vii
   I. Introduction   1
  II. *Robinson Crusoe*: Author and Narrator   20
 III. *Captain Singleton*: Puritan and Picaresque   48
  IV. *Moll Flanders*: Parodies of Respectability   75
   V. *A Journal of the Plague Year*:
      Fact and Fiction   107
  VI. *Colonel Jack*: Heroic and Mock-Heroic   126
 VII. *Roxana*: The Verbal World   155
Index   189

Preface

This study focuses on Defoe's novels, the major works
of fiction that he published between 1719 and 1724. Some
would deny that these works are novels, calling them
instead precursors to the novel. In any case, they are
closely related to the literary form that we now call
the novel. I have given readings of these works, and
have attempted to define some of the traditions—literary, intellectual, and religious—to which they are
related.

Defoe's adaptations of various subliterary forms of
seventeenth- and early-eighteenth-century writing
made these forms available to the novel. The diary,
spiritual autobiography, criminal biography and autobiography, travel story, picaresque adventure, and historical narrative are among the forms that he
transformed into the new fiction. The religious element
is centrally important to all these transformations.
Defoe exploited the psychological potentialities of conventional religious notions—fear, guilt, agonies of repentance, and wrestlings with conscience. When he organized an adventure story according to a religious pattern,
he emphasized the contradictions and congruences
between the inner and outer worlds. The focus of the
story is then no longer external alone: the central figure
becomes a character and not merely someone to identify
with or to excoriate.

Defoe's position early in the novelistic tradition encourages us to see him as the clumsy but useful forerunner of less naïve practitioners of fiction. There is another way to see him. He was writing near the beginning of one tradition but at the height of another—the satiric. And he was an accomplished writer long before he began writing novels: for many years he had dealt with the rhetorical problems of writing both satire and nonfictional prose. I have attempted to see Defoe's novels in relation to other eighteenth-century novels, and I have attempted to see them also in the context in which Defoe was writing, a context that did not include our conception of the novel.

It is a mistake, I think, to see Defoe's novels as meticulously organized in relation to some purpose—but it is also a mistake to see them as mighty mazes without plans. They are informed by a mind of considerable intelligence and coherence. Segments of Defoe's novels often seem designed to illustrate moral platitudes, but when one of his novels is considered as a whole, the various morals are sometimes neither clear nor entirely compatible with each other. Some readers have, in consequence, been led to deny any coherent structure to Defoe's novels. However, the pseudo-autobiographical form that Defoe used, as well as the haste with which he wrote, suggests that his novels should be read as explorations, not only as demonstrations. He shaped his characters, but in a sense he was also pursuing them through varying circumstances and degrees of consistency. Sometimes we discover as much about Defoe by attempting to define what he learned as by explaining what he wished to teach us.

Defoe often goes to considerable lengths to detach himself from his narrative. No major character is ever consistently his spokesman. However, Defoe as author leaves behind traces of himself. He never fully disguises the machinery of his fiction: he never completely eliminates the verbal detritus that betrays the process of composing the novel. The process of writing has, in Defoe, a meaning that is in addition to the written. This additional meaning belongs both to the novel and to biography. I have attempted to trace a process of change in Defoe's moral and literary assumptions. This process is revealed intermittently and not entirely consistently; nevertheless, it is a part of the meaning of his novels and of his life.

It is easy to emphasize Defoe's intellectual limitations. But even a brief study of the variety of his writings—satire, literary criticism, economics, moral and political philosophy—reveals a man of wide reading who was keenly interested in the central issues of his time. He was by no means a scholar, but neither did he live in an intellectual vacuum, untouched by the ideas of his contemporaries.

My task is both limited and comprehensive. I am assessing only a small portion of Defoe's achievement, but I am attempting to consider that portion intensively, pursuing a variety of concerns. My indebtedness to many works of scholarship is apparent—studies of Defoe, the novel, satire, and the eighteenth-century social and historical context. Here I will mention only a few of the works having the most direct bearing on my subject.

Two biographical works are indispensable: James Sutherland, *Defoe* (2d ed., New York: Barnes and Noble, 1950); John Robert Moore, *Daniel Defoe: Citizen of the Modern World* (Chicago: University of Chicago Press, 1958). Sutherland has also published a general critical study surveying Defoe's entire career: *Daniel Defoe: A Critical Study* (Cambridge, Mass.: Harvard University Press, 1971). Of the more specialized studies of Defoe, the following are closely related to my study: J. Paul Hunter, *The Reluctant Pilgrim: Defoe's Emblematic*

Method and Quest for Form in Robinson Crusoe (Baltimore: The Johns Hopkins University Press, 1966); Maximillian Novak, *Defoe and the Nature of Man* (New York: Oxford University Press, 1963); George A. Starr, *Defoe and Spiritual Autobiography* (Princeton: Princeton University Press, 1965), and *Defoe and Casuistry* (Princeton: Princeton University Press, 1971). Hunter shows that Defoe and his readers were accustomed to conceiving of narrative in emblematic terms. Novak documents the extent of Defoe's reading and his intellectual concerns. In his earlier book, Starr shows how the conventions of spiritual autobiography shaped Defoe's novels; and in his later book, he discusses the background and effects of Defoe's, and his characters', concern for rationalizing difficult moral choices.

A number of studies that are not primarily of Defoe suggest important contexts in which to consider him. Ian Watt, *The Rise of the Novel* (Berkeley and Los Angeles: University of California Press, 1957) is indispensable for anyone attempting to define the problems of writing novels when there were no novels. Ronald Paulson, *Satire and the Novel in Eighteenth-Century England* (New Haven: Yale University Press, 1967), examines the process of the absorption of satire by the novel. Pat Rogers, *Grub Street: Studies in a Subculture* (London: Methuen, 1972), restores a specificity to the term "Grub Street," a term that, to the modern reader, is rarely more than a vague metaphor in Swift and Pope.

Parts of this book were first published elsewhere, and are here reprinted in revised form. Much of Chapter II first appeared in *ELH* 38 (Sept. 1971), 377-396, under the title "Defoe and Crusoe," and is reprinted with the permission of The Johns Hopkins University Press. Much of Chapter V first appeared in *PMLA* 87 (May

1972), 417-423, under the title "H.F.'s Meditations: *A Journal of the Plague Year*," and is reprinted with the permission of the Modern Language Association. Some of Chapter VII first appeared in *Essays in Criticism* 21 (July, 1971), 227-235, under the title "Language and Character in Defoe's *Roxana*," and is reprinted with the permission of the editors.

Much of the first draft of this book was written during a leave from teaching made possible by a Summer Faculty Fellowship from the University of California, Santa Barbara. The Committee on Research of the Academic Senate at the University of California, Santa Barbara, granted funds for research and clerical assistance.

I am grateful for the many helpful suggestions of friends, editors, and the publisher's readers. I am especially grateful to George Starr, Frederick Turner, and Muriel Zimmerman, who read the manuscript in one or several of its earlier stages and provided essential criticism and encouragement.

I

Introduction

Daniel Defoe (1660-1731) is remembered primarily for works written late in his life and over a period of only five years. His first novel, *Robinson Crusoe*, was published in 1719; his last, *Roxana*, in 1724. His life was almost as varied as that of one of his fictional heroes: among other things, he was satirist, journalist, businessman, and political agent. One cannot speak in a strict sense of Defoe's career: that word implies an inapplicable coherence.

Defoe's works are often evaluated in terms closely related to the attitudes that are adopted toward his life. When he is regarded as a literary hack, an exemplar of the Grub Street "modern," his works are judged to be, at best, competent journalism or pseudojournalism, devised for the moment and having little but historical interest. When he is regarded as the originator of the novel, the major literary form of the modern world, new subtleties are discovered. Defoe was of course both hack and innovator. We should remember the multitude of literary historians who have demonstrated that Defoe's was a limited talent. We should remember also that Defoe interested Virginia Woolf, André Gide, and Franz Kafka, among many others.

Our difficulty in placing Defoe may result in part from the way in which the Tory satirists, especially Swift and Pope, have shaped our attitudes toward the eighteenth century: they abominated the writers of popular

1

literature and political journalists for hire. This moralistic perspective perhaps leads us to ignore the fact that Defoe shared much of the intellectual world of Swift and Pope. The range of his reading, of his knowledge of the intellectual issues of his time, is suggested by Maximillian Novak: "As a child of his age, Defoe formulated his own scheme of natural law, and by borrowing, combining, and emphasizing various concepts in the writings of Grotius, Hobbes, Locke, and many other philosophers, he was able to achieve a certain eclectic originality."[1]

The affinities between Defoe's works and the works of the Augustan satirists are as important as the more obvious differences. The characters of Defoe's novels are created by a mass of external information, but their internal principles of coherence remain obscure. They impose varying patterns of explanation upon their lives in order to supply coherence and integrity where none is apparent. These characters are novelistic counterparts to the central figures in Augustan satire. A brief excursion into Augustan satire and into some of its intellectual background is relevant to a definition of Defoe's achievement.

Both Swift and Pope present characters who, like Defoe's, are authenticated by a mass of detail. But the characters of Augustan satire collapse; they are shown to be deceivers without "character" at all.[2] Perhaps the salient example is the poet of *The Dunciad*, who, while fleeing from the booksellers, is divested of his attributes:

[1] *Defoe and the Nature of Man* (New York: Oxford University Press, 1963), p. 2; and passim, for further suggestions about the extent of Defoe's reading in philosophy and law.

[2] See Hugh Kenner, *The Counterfeiters* (Bloomington: Indiana University Press, 1968), for a study of "the esthetic of the counterfeiter" in the eighteenth century and later. Kenner comments on the interest in simulations of men.

And now the victor stretch'd his eager hand
Where the tall Nothing stood, or seem'd to stand;
A shapeless shade, it melted from his sight,
Like forms in clouds, or visions of the night.
To seize his papers, Curl, was next thy care;
His papers light, fly diverse, tost in air;
Songs, sonnets, epigrams the winds uplift,
And whisk 'em back to Evans, Young, and Swift.
Th' embroider'd suit at least he deem'd his prey;
That suit an unpay'd taylor snatch'd away.
No rag, no scrap, of all the beau, or wit,
That once so flutter'd, and that once so writ.
                                    (II, ll. 109-120)

Swift's modest proposer too seems at first substantial. He is earnest and consistent; he has a wife past child-bearing and an acquaintance from America. But the work makes sense only when we finally see the creator's opposition to his creature: the proposer disintegrates, becoming a comic tool in a didactic fiction.

The Memoirs of Martinus Scriblerus—as Charles Kerby-Miller remarks, "a most exceptionally valuable document for the study of attitudes and beliefs" in the early eighteenth century—presents this elusive satiric character in more explicitly philosophical terms.[3] The *Memoirs* contains a plan for the creation of a man who needs only someone to wind him up weekly:

---

[3] *Memoirs of the Extraordinary Life, Works, and Discoveries of Martinus Scriblerus*, ed. Charles Kerby-Miller (New Haven: Yale University Press, 1950), p. viii. All references to the *Memoirs* are to the same edition.

The Members of the Scriblerus Club included Pope, Swift, Gay, Arbuthnot, Parnell, and Robert Harley, who was Defoe's employer.

See Robert A. Erickson, "Situations of Identity in the *Memoirs of Martinus Scriblerus*," *MLQ* 26 (1965), 388-400, for a relevant discussion.

... we have employ'd one of our Members, a great
Virtuoso at Nuremberg, to make a sort of an Hy-
draulic Engine, in which a chemical liquor resembling Blood, is driven through elastic chanels resembling arteries and veins, by the force of an
Embolus like the heart, and wrought by a pneu-
matic Machine of the nature of the lungs, with ropes
and pullies, like the nerves, tendons and muscles:
And we are persuaded that this our artificial Man
will not only walk, and speak, and perform most
of the outward actions of the animal life, but (being
wound up once a week) will perhaps reason as well
as most of your Country Parsons (p. 141).

The intellectual issues raised by the *Memoirs* were
prominent ones in the second decade of the eighteenth
century. The Scriblerians persistently attack what are,
from a commonsensical point of view, the absurdities
of systematic philosophy. They use the plan for an
artificial man to mock, among other things, philosophical substitutions of mechanical operations for the
spirit. Earlier in the chapter that culminates in this
projected mechanical man, Martinus Scriblerus tries to
find the "Seat of the Soul"; finally, like Descartes, "he
grew fond of the *Glandula Pinealis*" (p. 137). He
then begins a series of dissections. The freethinkers
find his bent for experimentation promising: "Is it not
Demonstration to a person of your Sense, that, since
you cannot find it, there is *no such thing*" (p. 138)? To
them, the search for a soul leads inevitably to the denial
of its existence. And if man is mechanical, a mechanical
man is like other men.

The larger issue behind the Augustan interest in
artificial man is that of personal identity. Is a man more
than the sum of his physical attributes? Is a simulated
man any different from other men? Traditional answers

to these questions posited souls and minds, units that somehow exist in conjunction with the body without being identical to it. But philosophical and scientific analysis presents a problem of synthesis. After a man's thoughts, sensations, body, and behavior are broken into their component parts, where are his mind and soul? If one puts together all the pieces, does one have a mind and soul—or can one have a man without these things? The question put more psychologically is whether or not there is a self. If a man is to be resurrected out of the rubble of his attributes, a self to which all the attributes may be referred is a convenience. It is necessary at least to assume a coherence, a sustained organizing principle that connects diversity. But to draw that organizing principle out of the mass of evidence may be difficult or impossible.

Defoe's novels raise the issue of self and identity prominently.[4] The form that Defoe adopts is the autobiographical memoir, in which his heroes try out many explanations of their lives, using the book as their final organizing device. The narrative is used to attest to there being more to the narrator's life than a meaningless flux of disparate experience. Autobiography becomes an attempt to create self and soul. Although Defoe is often ironical about these characters, his stance is never merely that of the external ironist. He sympathetically depicts the plight that the satirists lash. His characters present their own cases and demand our sympathy. We are not put in the position of detached

[4] See Homer O. Brown, "The Displaced Self in the Novels of Daniel Defoe," *ELH* 38 (1971), 562-590, for a valuable discussion of the nature of "self" in Defoe's novels and of the possible inferences that can be drawn about Defoe from these novels: "Secrecy seems to be an absolute precondition of self-revelation . . . these narrators seem to be under a double compulsion to expose and to conceal themselves." (p. 563)

observers who overlook the instructive collapse of a
puppet. Instead, we observe a character's desperate
efforts to pull himself together in extremely difficult
circumstances. And all Defoe's central characters, except Roxana, succeed in doing this. They avoid being
stripped to a presumptive but nonexistent core. Nevertheless, the reader is made aware of the suppressions
that are necessary if these characters are to reduce
disparate experiences and chaotic impulses to some
chosen order.

In Defoe's time, the principal philosophical discussion
of the problem of personal identity was Locke's in *An
Essay Concerning Human Understanding* (1690).
Defoe, like many educated men of his time, was well
acquainted with the works of Locke. He used Locke's
ideas in his political poem *Jure Divino*; he also mentioned Locke in the *Review*; on one occasion, he took
up the question of "Whether a dog may not properly
be said to think on things past and to come," a question
that had its roots in Locke's attempt to define man.
Maximillian Novak has also shown that Locke had an
influence on Defoe's conception of fiction and on some
of the political and economic ideas in *Robinson Crusoe.*[5]

Locke accepts the view that matter is continuously
changing: over the course of a lifetime, we are different
substances but have the same identity. Although Locke

[5] See Kenneth MacLean, *John Locke and English Literature of
the Eighteenth Century* (New Haven: Yale University Press, 1936),
for a discussion of Locke's influence.

See Defoe's *Review* III, 429b, and *Review* II, 39a, for his references
to Locke. The following sections of Locke's *Essay* are relevant to
Defoe's discussion of a dog's powers of thought: II, ix, 12; II, x,
10; II, xi, 7. See also MacLean, pp. 68-81.

See Maximillian Novak, "Defoe's Theory of Fiction," *SP* 61 (1964),
650-668; and "Robinson Crusoe and Economic Utopia," *Kenyon
Review* 25 (1963), 474-490, for discussions of Locke's influence on
Defoe.

leaves open the question of the materiality of the soul, he argues that personal identity consists in something other than a continuing substance—consciousness:

> to find wherein personal identity consists, we must consider what *person* stands for; which, I think, is a thinking intelligent being, that has reason and reflection, and can consider itself as itself, the same thinking thing, in different times and places; which it does only by the *consciousness* which is inseparable from thinking, and, as it seems to me, essential to it: it being impossible for any one to perceive without *perceiving* that he does perceive (II, xxvii, 11).

> ... it being the same consciousness that makes a man be himself to himself, personal identity depends on that only, whether it be annexed solely to one individual substance, or can be continued in a succession of several substances (II, xxvii, 10).[6]

The *Spectator* disseminated many of Locke's ideas, including a summary of his discussion of personal identity. The account in the *Spectator* contained this quotation of Locke:

> Had I the same consciousness that I saw the ark and Noah's flood, as that I saw an overflowing of the Thames last winter, or as that I write now, I could no more doubt that I who write this now, that saw the Thames overflowed last winter, and that viewed the flood at the general deluge, was the same *self*—place that self in what *substance* you please—than that I who write this am the same

[6] Quotations of Locke are from *An Essay Concerning Human Understanding,* ed. Alexander Campbell Fraser (Oxford: Clarendon Press, 1894). All references are to the book, chapter, and paragraph of Locke's *Essay.*

myself now whilst I write (whether I consist of all the same substance, material or immaterial, or no) that I was yesterday (II, xxvii, 16; quoted in *Spectator*, no. 578, Aug. 9, 1714).

A story follows in the *Spectator* about a continuing identity in different bodies: a king, tricked by a dervish into entering the body of a deer, later enters a nightingale to be near his queen, and eventually enters her lapdog. This is not what Locke had in mind of course, but the story at least hints at something that Locke does not consider—the anguish resulting from an identity that is in conflict with one's physical condition. Surely Locke's hypothetical man who is conscious of having observed the flood will also question his own notions of a self; he may doubt his own coherence, and wonder whether that self might not be duplicitous.

Locke's solution to a philosophical issue raises obvious religious and psychological questions. By linking a man's actions one to another only by memory, Locke resolves the issue of personal identity but only exacerbates the related one of personal integrity. Several scattered comments show that Locke recognizes some of the unsettling implications of his solution; his philosophy, however, does not require him to deal with these implications. "But is not a man drunk or sober the same person? Why else is he punished for the fact he commits when drunk, though he be never afterwards conscious of it" (II, xxvii, 22)? Locke concludes that this problem for human justice can be resolved only "in the Great Day, wherein the secrets of all hearts shall be laid open."

Locke then considers the possibility of "two distinct incommunicable consciousnesses acting the same body, the one constantly by day, the other by night" (II, xxvii, 23). Are they not, he asks, "two as distinct persons as Socrates and Plato?" But what happens to personal identity in a man with a bad memory:

For, granting that the thinking substance in man must be necessarily supposed immaterial, it is evident that immaterial thinking thing may sometimes part with its past consciousness, and be restored to it again: as appears in the forgetfulness men often have of their past actions; and the mind many times recovers the memory of a past consciousness, which it had lost for twenty years together. Make these intervals of memory and forgetfulness to take their turns regularly by day and night, and you have two persons with the same immaterial spirit, as much as in the former instance two persons with the same body (II, xxvii, 23).

Locke remains consistent, but anyone who takes the problem personally as well as philosophically may be disturbed by the possibility of being two persons. But Locke does not admit even a partial communication between the two persons. Consequently he need not even consider the psychological problem of two differing but incompletely separated consciousnesses—what in an extreme form we call schizophrenia.

The Scriblerians too take up the problem of consciousness. The satirized freethinkers in *The Memoirs of Martinus Scriblerus* wish to prove that everything can be explained by mechanics; therefore they argue against the Lockean notion that consciousness exists apart from substance. The freethinkers write of their opponents: "One of their chief Arguments is that *Self-consciousness* cannot inhere in any system of Matter, because all matter is made up of several distinct beings, which never can make up one individual thinking being" (p. 138). Against this view, the freethinkers argue: "Consciousness, with its several modes of sensation, intellection, volition, etc. . . . is the result from the mechanical composition of the whole Animal" (p. 139). Just put the material pieces together, they say, and there is no need to worry about some immaterial piece.

Although the Scriblerians are attacking the free-thinkers, they are, in addition, attacking systematic philosophy. A silly discussion of mechanical consciousness is attributed by the Scriblerians to the freethinkers, but it redounds not only against the freethinkers but also against the Lockeans:

> They make a great noise about this Individuality: how a man is conscious to himself that he is the same Individual he was twenty years ago; notwithstanding the flux state of the Particles of matter that compose his body. We think this is capable of a very plain answer, and may be easily illustrated by a familiar example.
>
> Sir John Cutler had a pair of black worsted stockings, which his maid darn'd so often with silk, that they became at last a pair of silk stockings. Now supposing those stockings of Sir John's endued with some degree of Consciousness at every particular darning, they would have been sensible, that they were the same individual pair of stockings both before and after the darning; and this sensation would have continued in them through all the succession of darnings; and yet after the last of all, there was not perhaps one thread left of the first pair of stockings, but they were grown to be silk stockings, as was said before (p. 140).

The freethinkers' foolishness is defined by their reduction of men to stockings, but the comic absurdity of this vehicle is also a mockery of the entire philosophical issue. Can we believe that bodies have nothing to do with consciousness—or with personal identity? Such a belief is as absurd as confusing silk stockings with worsted ones. Our sense of ourselves is inextricably bound up with our bodies and our surroundings. To examine the Scriblerians too closely is of course to become their victim. Nevertheless, the Scriblerian attack on these freethinkers does reveal the strains engendered by Locke's explanation of personal identity.

Hume's discussion of the problem in his *Treatise of Human Nature* (1739-40) exposes the skeptical conclusion that was implicit in Locke's arguments: identity is a comforting fiction that we are unwilling to abandon:

> In order to justify to ourselves this absurdity, we often feign some new and unintelligible principle, that connects the objects together and prevents their interruption or variation. Thus we feign the continued existence of the perception of our senses to remove the interruption, and run into the notion of a *soul* and *self* and *substance* to disguise the variation.[7]

Self, says Hume, is only "a bundle or collection of different perceptions, which succeed each other with an inconceivable rapidity and are in a perpetual flux and movement" (p. 174). Although memory is the source of our notions of identity, it imposes a unity that does not exist: "... identity is nothing really belonging to these different perceptions and uniting them together; but is merely a quality which we attribute to them because of the union of their ideas in the imagination when we reflect upon them." (p. 181). Locke's explanation of personal identity is here severely limited: Hume implies that the consciousness linking the disparate parts of our life is itself only one of the disparate parts. Furthermore, we remember very little:

> For how few of our past actions are there of which we have any memory? Who can tell me, for in-

[7] *The Philosophy of David Hume*, ed. V. C. Chappel (New York: Random House, 1963), p. 176. All references to Hume's *Treatise* are to Book I, Part IV, Section VI, "Of Personal Identity."

stance, what were his thoughts and actions on the
first of January 1715, the 11th of March 1719, and
the 3rd of August 1733? ... It will be incumbent
on those who affirm that memory produces entirely
our personal identity to give a reason why we can
thus extend our identity beyond our memory (pp.
182-183).

As Hume recognized, one might agree with him that
"The identity which we ascribe to the mind of man is
only a fictitious one" (p. 180) without being any the
less impelled to create the fiction. The philosophical
arguments question too many notions that we find it
difficult to do without. Nevertheless, in the early eighteenth century the problem of personal identity was felt
to be an important one, and the discussion was not
limited to philosophers. Empirical science as well as
philosophy raises the issue, theologians take it up, it
appears in the pages of the *Spectator*, and it is prominent
in Augustan satire. All this is not to argue that Defoe's
novels must be read as precise exemplars of a Lockean,
or any other, philosophical position. Defoe and the
philosophers are dealing with problems that have general human implications, and Defoe in his novels does
not deal with these problems in a specifically philosophical way. However, knowing the prominence of the
contemporary discussions of personal identity and the
extent of Defoe's reading, we have no reasonable
grounds for positing a simpleminded Defoe with a simpleminded conception of character.

The reader of Defoe's biography may feel that Defoe's
concern with problems of identity needs no external
explanation. Much of his life, and especially that part
of it just before he began writing novels, seems to be
in desperate need of an explanation that will impart
some principle of coherence to it. Defoe's life for several

years after the death of Queen Anne in 1714 is compared by James Sutherland to the life of a "badger, a creature that comes out in the dark, and avoids the more dangerous daylight."[8] A staunch Whig under King William, Defoe became a secret-agent of Harley, Queen Anne's moderate Tory minister. Then, after Queen Anne's death and the Hanoverian accession, he is thought to have been secretly employed by Whigs. The usual charge of unscrupulous political opportunism is undeniable but perhaps of no great significance; Defoe often found plausible explanations for what he did. Nevertheless, the curious and tangled roles that he seems to have been playing shortly before the writing of his novels have a psychological interest that exceeds their political importance.

From probably 1717 until 1720, Defoe was, among other things, writing for *Mist's Weekly Journal*, a Tory paper that strenuously opposed the Whig government. Defoe is thought to have had two employers: Mist and the Whig government. His task for the government was to tone down the attacks of the opposition. Put another way, his task was to attack the government in milder terms than others might presumably use. One assumes that Mist employed him at least in part because he was a good writer; he wrote interesting attacks on the government. One wonders if Defoe was always certain about which side he was on? In any case, the Whig government had some doubts about Defoe's position: twice during Defoe's time with the *Weekly Journal*, the paper was investigated by the government. In 1718 Mist and the printer were examined about an article that was attributed to Defoe. Finally in 1729 Mist was

[8] *Defoe* (2d ed., New York: Barnes and Noble, 1950), p. 204. See Sutherland's chapter "Mist's Man," pp. 204-206, for an account of this portion of Defoe's life.

pilloried and imprisoned for another article. Immediately after this article's appearance, Defoe, presumably frightened, denied that he had written it and blamed Mist.

The possibilities for duplicities within duplicities in Defoe's association with Mist are perhaps extreme, but not uncharacteristic. Defoe was also at this same time performing similar services for the Whig government in *Dormer's News-Letter* and *Mercurius Politicus*. And he had previously done the same thing for the Tories: before Queen Anne's death, he had been softening the attacks of a Whig journal, the *Flying Post*, on the Tory government. In 1714 he had been prosecuted for accusing a Tory peer, Lord Anglesby, of being a Jacobite. Defoe's intricate double roles inevitably subjected him to misinterpretation, and one may have difficulty distinguishing role from reality. He played contradictory roles with remarkable vigor.

The Shortest Way with the Dissenters (1702) and the misunderstandings it occasioned suggest that the difficulties of placing Defoe are to be found in his method of writing as well as in his behavior.[9] The widespread failure of his early readers to grasp his satire of the High Church Tory party, the High-Flyers, is sometimes taken as evidence of Defoe's miscalculation and at other

---

[9] Wayne Booth, *The Rhetoric of Fiction* (Chicago: University of Chicago Press, 1961), deals with this problem in Defoe, Swift, and other writers in the section of his book entitled "Troubles with Irony in Earlier Literature," pp. 316-323.

E. Anthony James, *Daniel Defoe's Many Voices: A Rhetorical Study of Prose Style and Literary Method* (Amsterdam: Editions Rodopi, 1972), is also relevant to this point. James deals with Defoe's varying styles, and sees in them evidence of a conscious literary method.

Leopold Damrosch, Jr., "Defoe as Ambiguous Impersonator," *MP* 71 (1973), comments that "Many of the ambiguities of Defoe as impersonator" still appear even in "prose works in which Defoe does not present a fiction" (p. 153).

times as evidence of his readers' stupidity. When the work is put into the perspective of literary history and classified as satire, we see Defoe's major intention clearly: he is without doubt attacking the High Church extremists. However, when the work first appeared, its intention was not so clear.

Defoe's method is to adopt the tone of a fanatical supporter of the established Church in order to expose the final ugly implications of the arguments against dissent. Defoe's narrator is an embarrassment to the High-Flyers; his rabid attacks on the dissenters and especially his Jacobitism, his reference to the "new *Hodgepodge of a Dutch-government"*—all are at the very least impolitic.[10] But what is a dissenter to make of this comment: "You have *Butcher'd* one King, *Depos'd* another King, and made a *mock King* of a Third; and yet you cou'd have the face to expect to be employ'd and trusted by a Fourth" (pp. 116-117). This remark seems better adapted to inflaming the hatred for the dissenters than to showing the absurdity of the already existing hatreds. And later the narrator comments on the ease of bringing the dissenters into the established Church: ". . . the Spirit of Martyrdom is over; they that will go to Church to be chosen Sheriffs and Mayors, would go to forty Churches rather than be Hang'd" (p. 128). This statement is, again, a strange one to put into a document that is designed to defend dissent. Defoe here is attacking occasional conformity just as sharply as he is attacking High Church fanaticism. Intelligent readers, High-Flyers or dissenters, might reasonably have been expected to be angered by *The Shortest Way*. Only those moderates who were detached from the controversy or those foolish High-

---

[10] *The Shortest Way with the Dissenters and Other Pamphlets* (Oxford: Basil Blackwell, 1927), p. 116. Subsequent references to this work are to the same edition.

Flyers who read the piece straightforwardly could possibly not be offended.

The problem is not Defoe's ineptitude. He could, and did, write satire that was understood—*The True-Born Englishman* (1701), for example. But the method of *The Shortest Way* led to comments that were not appropriate to a limited satiric purpose. Despite his ultimate intention, Defoe wrote a fanatical attack on the dissenters, not an ironical defense of them. The narrator attacks the dissenters not only where they are most easily defended but also where they are vulnerable. The author adopts a role and plays it consistently, even when the role is not efficiently adapted to his ostensible purpose. He chooses to accept the limitations of his narrator rather than those of his purpose.

In some respects, Defoe's method resembles Swift's. For example, *A Modest Proposal* leads the reader plausibly into a discussion of an economic problem and then presents him with a mad solution. The reader who bought and read this unsigned economic tract on its first appearance in Dublin in 1729 must have been angered by the putative author. One who took thé tract seriously was revolted; one who did not, surely felt swindled. But in either case, Swift's reader was made aware of "other Expedients" than the narrator's. Swift chose a fiction that would alienate the reader, one that would not even appear to seduce a normal man. Although the modest proposer is as consistent as Defoe's High-Flyer, Swift's satire alludes far more pronouncedly than Defoe's to a set of values differing from the narrator's. Both Swift and Pope declare their judgments on their characters. Their simulated men refer the reader to an author who is diagnosing a moral illness. However, Defoe's simulation is not so transparent; his High-Flyer does not so obviously collapse into the author's symbol of evil.

The satiric method of *The Shortest Way with the Dissenters* and the novelistic method of *Robinson Crusoe* are related. In neither work is the author insistently present. It is not that author and character are always indistinguishable, even within the confines of the work itself: in both cases, one senses an author who diverges from his character. Nevertheless, these divergences are not precisely defined. The author seems to be playing a role, that of his character, in which a more complicated self is occasionally disclosed.

In the course of writing his novels, Defoe's technical skill increased. He had long been a competent satiric ironist, but in writing novels he had a new problem.[11] He had to present a seemingly autonomous central character while at the same time marking his judgments of the character. If the character is not of interest for its own sake, the work becomes a satiric symbol of its author's opinions; if the character is not evaluated, the work loses its moral coherence. In *Moll Flanders, Colonel Jack,* and *Roxana*, Defoe demonstrates that he can achieve a generally coherent ironic perspective on vividly realized characters. However, this aspect of Defoe's technical achievement is in many ways irrelevant to the value of his works. *Roxana* is in some respects a different work from *Robinson Crusoe*, but it does not deal with fundamentally different concerns; nor is *Roxana* necessarily a better work. Defoe's central achievement from *Robinson Crusoe* to *Roxana* is the same: with great power and some precision, he presents characters who have been taught to assume souls but have difficulty in finding them. His ironic perspective sometimes lends precision but rarely power.

[11] See Maximillian Novak, "Defoe's Use of Irony," in *The Uses of Irony*, Papers on Defoe and Swift Read at a Clark Library Seminar (Los Angeles: William Andrews Clark Memorial Library Seminar papers, 1966).

The son of a dissenter and educated for the Presby-
terian ministry, Defoe was well fitted to feel the strains
of both his new life and the new philosophy. His Puritan
tradition emphasized man's solitude in an alien world;[12]
more specifically, the institutions of Church and state
(Defoe was born in the year of the Restoration) could
provide no order for a devout dissenter's life. His tradition gave him little external support, but demanded that
he examine the soul that the philosophers were having
difficulty finding.

Defoe's adaptation of spiritual autobiography for his
novelistic purposes suggests both his religious perspective and the difficulties of maintaining it.[13] Devout
Christians of the seventeenth century kept diaries in
which they recorded their daily activities: from these
diaries they sometimes drew the information for a spiritual autobiography. In the events of daily life, they
discerned an informing principle: God's providential
order. Defoe's characters try to find this spiritual meaning, but the material of their lives is extremely stubborn.
Defoe's novels reveal the discordancies of mind that
result from a life having only a dubious relationship
either to an inner principle or to a stable external one.

Biography, contemporary philosophy, and literary

[12] See Cynthia Griffin Wolff, "Literary Reflections of the Puritan
Character," JHI 29 (1968), 13-32, for a succinct discussion of the
Puritan sense of isolation. See also Ian Watt, *The Rise of the Novel*
(Berkeley and Los Angeles: University of California Press, 1957),
especially the chapter "Robinson Crusoe: Individualism and the
Novel," pp. 60-92, for comments on the relationship of the sacred
and the secular in Puritanism.

[13] See George A. Starr, *Defoe and Spiritual Autobiography* (Princeton: Princeton University Press, 1965), for a discussion of Defoe's
use of this form. See also J. Paul Hunter, *The Reluctant Pilgrim:
Defoe's Emblematic Method and Quest for Form in Robinson
Crusoe* (Baltimore: Johns Hopkins Press, 1966), for discussions of
the influence of other kinds of Puritan religious writings on Defoe.

form—all help to define the nature of Defoe's fiction. But the question of Defoe's understanding, of his intention, remains. Did he see the implications of his own fiction? Is he analyst or exemplar of his society's condition? Such questions about Defoe can never be answered precisely, but they are, nevertheless, inescapable: the writer's relationship to what is written is part of its meaning. The development of Defoe's fictional technique gives us, I think, a guide to the quality of his understanding of the issues raised by his novels. Defoe returns repeatedly to similar characters and similar issues, but his authorial position changes: he gradually introduces himself as an implied ironic presence. The line of development from work to work is not precise, but there is unmistakably a change. Defoe's developing irony reveals his clearer understanding of the failures not only of his characters but also of the values by which they are judged. In *Roxana*, Defoe finally shows the collapse of values to which he himself must have adhered or pretended. His irony is negative; he substitutes no new values for the old ones. For Defoe, the writing of novels seems to have been, among many other things, an act of clarification. Ceasing to write novels may have been his response to unwelcome knowledge.

II

Robinson Crusoe: Author and Narrator

The Life and Strange Surprizing Adventures of Robinson Crusoe was published in 1719. According to the title page, it was "written by Himself"; the "preface" mentions, in addition, an editor. The work purports to be autobiography, and was lent at least a limited plausibility by the contemporary interest in Alexander Selkirk, a sailor who spent five years alone on an uninhabited island. Defoe's relationship to his book is difficult to define because of his narrative method: he tries to authenticate the account as being entirely Crusoe's. Questions arise: Does Defoe have any discernible attitude toward his character? Or is Defoe perhaps quite literally writing the book that Crusoe would have written? These questions are impelled by the narrative inefficiency of *Robinson Crusoe*: the book is filled with events, but it does not move along easily. It contains many seeming irrelevancies, contradictions, and underdeveloped suggestions. Are these to be dismissed or interpreted? The manner in which the story is written suggests characteristics of its writer. Are these to be referred to Crusoe or to Defoe? Often the meaning of the narrative seems not to be presented but to be escaping.

Charles Gildon raised the relevant issues in 1719. He imagined a meeting between Defoe and Crusoe:

D[anie]l. Why, ye airy Fantoms, are you not my Creatures? mayn't I make of you what I please?

Cru[soe]. Why, yes, you may make of us what you please; but when you raise Beings contradictory to common Sense, and destructive of Religion and Morality; they will rise up against you. . . .[1]

Is this "strange whimsical, inconsistent Being,"[2] who writes the book and expounds its morality, Defoe's creature or only his pseudonym? Unfortunately Gildon was interested only in using Crusoe as an example of Defoe's muddles and pretensions—his pamphlet becomes a dreary, though often accurate, catalog of the deficiencies of "Mr. D[aniel] De F[oe], of London, Hosier,"[3] as revealed in his book *Robinson Crusoe*.

Defoe defended himself against Gildon in a collection of moral essays, which he published as *Serious Reflections during the Life and Surprising Adventures of Robinson Crusoe*. His responses to Gildon in this work only complicate the question of his relation to Crusoe. Defoe has Crusoe insist on his own autonomy with an obstinacy that is, at least in retrospect, comic. One may of course dismiss this oddity by citing economic motives: Crusoe's name will help to sell Defoe's old moral essays. But explaining a motive does not necessarily define a performance. Defoe, well known as the author of *Robinson Crusoe*, wrote "Robinson Crusoe's Preface" to a collection of religious essays: "I, Robinson Crusoe, being at this time in perfect and sound mind and memory, thanks be to God therefore, do hereby declare their

---

[1] "A Dialogue Betwixt D[aniel] F[o]e, Robinson Crusoe and his Man Friday," from *Robinson Crusoe Examin'd and Criticis'd*, ed. Paul Dottin (London: J. M. Dent, 1923), p. 69.

[2] Gildon, p. 70.

[3] Gildon, p. 63.

objection ['that it is all formed and embellished by invention to impose upon the world'] is an invention scandalous in design, and false in fact. . . ."[4] But Crusoe then goes on to hint that the truth about himself is somehow related to the truth about Daniel Defoe: ". . . there is not a circumstance in the imaginary story but has its just allusion to a real story" (pp. xi-xii). The introduction to this volume of serious reflections is an entirely transparent equivocation: Crusoe is alive because he is independent of an author, but he is true because he is Defoe.

An author whose actions so bristle with contradictions cannot easily be brought proximate to his creature. One can begin with what author and putative author indubitably share: the language of their common book. "I cannot explain by any possible Energy of Words" is the introduction to a passage about Crusoe's loneliness.[5] In the subsequent account there is no illusion of emotion. We are given this sample of Crusoe's "breaking out": "O that there had been but one or two; nay, or but one Soul sav'd out of this Ship, to have escap'd to me, that I might but have had one Companion, one Fellow-Creature to have spoken to me, and to have convers'd with" (p. 188)! This highly rhetorical passage is addressed to no one except the hypothetical reader. It is followed by an analysis of Crusoe's emotions, which are without fictional reality.

The inadequacies of elevated language are especially

[4] *Serious Reflections during the Life and Surprising Adventures of Robinson Crusoe*, ed. George Aitken (London: J. M. Dent, 1895), p. ix.

[5] *Robinson Crusoe*, ed. J. Donald Crowley (New York: Oxford University Press, 1972). References to *The Farther Adventures of Robinson Crusoe* are to Volumes XII and XIII of the Shakespeare Head Edition of the Novels and Selected Writings of Daniel Defoe (Oxford, 1927). All subsequent references to *Robinson Crusoe* are in the text.

apparent in the conversion episodes. Crusoe's undescribed "broken and imperfect Prayer" (p. 94) does not
lead to his later ecstatic shout by any progression that
we can easily regard as spiritually authentic: *"Jesus,
thou Son of David, Jesus, thou exalted, Prince and
Saviour, give me Repentance"* (p. 96)! Fever and his
loathsome concoctions of tobacco explain Crusoe's rhetoric more plausibly than does repentance. Later Crusoe
decides that he cannot recommend his remedies: ". . .
I had frequent Convulsions in my Nerves and Limbs
for some Time" (p. 97).

The issue is not one of morals: we do not have to
decide either that Defoe is being ironic or that he is
a hypocrite. He attempts to create, as well as to explain,
the emotions that he assumes are Crusoe's. Defoe's
attempts to capture emotions are apparent not only in
the elevated diction but also in various quantitative
increases in the language, such as lists and repetitions.
The priest in *The Farther Adventures* speaks in several
languages to express his spiritual ecstasy (XIII, 39). But
the grandiose speeches that are intended to create
emotion only signify its absence.

As words inexorably slide away from their intended
signification, Defoe and Crusoe attempt to fix the emotion in gesture:

> I believe it is impossible to express to the Life what
> the Extasies and Transports of the Soul are, when
> it is so sav'd. . . . I walk'd about on the Shore, lifting
> up my Hands, and my whole Being, as I may say,
> wrapt up in the Contemplation of my Deliverance,
> making a Thousand Gestures and Motions which
> I cannot describe (p. 46).

In this book, actions are assumed to have an undeniable
reality even if they cannot be definitely described: the
more direct and authentic the emotion, the more likely

that discursive speech will be suppressed. Recognizing his father, "*Friday* kiss'd him, embrac'd him, hugg'd him, cry'd, laugh'd, hollow'd, jump'd about, danc'd, sung, then cry'd again, wrung his Hands, beat his own Face, and Head, and then sung, and jump'd about again, like a distracted Creature" (p. 238).

Both author and narrator are suspicious of language: it is at times a limitation that they wish to evade. But the psychic reality that appears beyond language is terrifying, and words are also often sought as a defense against fears. Those emotions authenticated by action often produce a state verging on madness. The similes implying a disturbed mind—Friday is "like a distracted Creature," and Crusoe runs about "like a Mad-man" (p. 47)—are literalized in the behavior of the passengers rescued at sea in *The Farther Adventures*: ". . . there were some in Tears, some raging, and tearing themselves, as if they had been in the greatest Agonies of Sorrow, some stark-raving and down-right lunatick, some ran about the Ship stamping with their Feet, others wringing their Hands . . . (XII, 128). . . . for if an Excess of Joy can carry men out to such a Length beyond the Reach of their Reason, what will not the Extravagancies of Anger, Rage, and a provok'd Mind carry us to" (XII, 131)? Intensities of emotion are conceived of as bizarre, uncontrollable, and damaging—a chaos within.

It is not surprising then that one finds a frequent retreat from such manifestations of feeling into language—a journal, lists, elaborate ritualistic bargaining (see p. 256). As much as possible, language itself is concretized. Unnecessary lists are written; though there is nothing with which to write, Crusoe wants the agreement with the Spaniards to be "put in writing" (p. 248); extreme gratitude for the Portuguese captain's kindness inspires a call "for a Pen and Ink to give him a Receipt" (p. 282). If unsatisfying as a simulator of high emotions, words nevertheless produce an order. Language is repressive of the fearsome inner energies and only obliquely expressive.[6]

We have moved from what Defoe and Crusoe share— the language of *Robinson Crusoe*—to what they may perhaps hold opposing notions of—the meaning of the language. Crusoe surveys his life of variety and misfortune with compassion, laughter, and sometimes an exceedingly cold eye. He comments both explicitly and implicitly—and sometimes not at all. But there is little sense of an author judging the narrator. *Robinson Crusoe* is ironic only in the limited sense that the narrator reveals his earlier moral blindness.

Traces of someone who is not a character do, nevertheless, remain; the author tries too blatantly to conceal himself. The twice-mentioned Pocket-Book (XIII, 138, 159), its "leaves rotted," is designed to vouch for the truth of the story and to excuse the omission of place names—but the verisimilitude of the travel book has already been rejected explicitly and repeatedly (XIII, 83, 109). Such declarations too are unnecessary after hundreds of pages have made clear that the narrative is an internal one about the eye *"never satisfied with Seeing"* (XIII, 110).

This sense of an incompletely hidden author appears frequently in the narrative machinery. The action of writing a book exists in the same way as the actions and evaluations of Crusoe—not only as the means for telling Crusoe's story but also as an adjunct to it. For example, when Crusoe flees, unjustly suspected of being

---

[6] Benjamin Boyce, "The Question of Emotion in Defoe," *SP* 50 (1953), 50, makes this comment on *Robinson Crusoe*: "Augustan reticence about the horrors has not prevented Defoe's twice giving us plain hints of what 'many dull things'—that is, what shocking, private, and indecorous things—would have gone into a stream-of-consciousness narrative."

a pirate, his letter of outraged innocence is summarized in the text. The letter contains no new information, and Crusoe goes on to note that "we had no Occasion ever to let the Pilot carry this Letter; for he never went back again" (XIII, 137). This is not Crusoe sorting out his life but an act of writing for its own sake, having a meaning independent of the narrative (I am not here arguing that narrative clumsiness is necessarily high art—only that it is not without meaning).

Crusoe uses the material world to obscure and control his destructive impulses. His behavior is not always entirely appropriate to the adventure that he is ostensibly recounting; nor is it always consonant with the moral scheme that he uses to shape his story. There is a blurring of outline, a sense that his actions fulfill psychic requirements neither directly expressed nor entirely moral or utilitarian. These indirections are similar to Defoe's. His writing is not always perfectly adapted to Crusoe: there are mannerisms serving a purpose not exclusively the character's.

Crusoe comments on his fortifications: "... as it appear'd afterward, there was no need of all this Caution from the Enemies that I apprehended Danger from" (p. 59). Subsequent events give us more confidence in Crusoe's hindsight than in Defoe's foresight: Defoe eliminates suspense about something to which his narrative persistently returns. Although concealment is essential to Crusoe's defense, fortifications never figure in it. Crusoe fortifies to restore his psychic equilibrium; whenever he has brought his defenses to seeming perfection, he is again disturbed. The many references to the fortified habitation culminate in a lengthy summarizing description (pp. 151-153). Immediately thereafter Crusoe sees the "Print of a Man's naked Foot" (p. 153). In his terror he first proposes to destroy all traces of his presence, but then he finds a better way to relieve his "Burthen of Anxiety" (p. 159): "... I resolv'd to draw me a second Fortification, in the same Manner of a Semicircle, at a Distance from my Wall just where I had planted a double Row of Trees about twelve years before, of which I made mention" (p. 161).

Descriptions of this habitation become a set piece in *Robinson Crusoe*—a result of Defoe's amplification as well as of Crusoe's elaboration. Defoe is finally obliged to assert the attractions of Crusoe's not entirely functional construction: he has the captain who rescues Crusoe express amazement at everything in Crusoe's life, "but above all the Captain admir'd my Fortification" (p. 258). In *The Farther Adventures*, the Spaniards explain their changes of it: Crusoe's old habitation has a dignity as a relic of a grander past. As Crusoe's dependents, the Spaniards are held to a more utilitarian standard of behavior than he was: Crusoe immediately inquires, "What put them upon all these Fortifications" (XII, 147)? By this time of course the attacks of savages have provided the justification previously missing.

Years before, the Spaniard had suggested wicker work for defense, but Crusoe "saw no Need of it" (p. 248). Defoe, however, rarely relinquishes a scrap of narrative material. Will Atkins, in many ways resembling the earlier Crusoe, lives in a wicker house that is described in an extended passage reminiscent of the descriptions of Crusoe's old habitation: Crusoe concludes, "Such a Piece of Basketwork, I believe, was never seen in the World, nor House, or Tent, so neatly contriv'd, much less, so built" (XII, 221). The author's unwillingness to give up anything is analogous to an important trait of his central figure. Crusoe attempts to salvage everything from the ship: "I had the biggest Magazin of all Kinds that ever were laid up, I believe, for one Man, but I was not Satisfy'd still; for while the Ship sat upright in that Posture, I thought I ought to get every

Thing out of her that I could" (p. 55). Crusoe first attempts to select from the ship that which will be useful; he then takes indiscriminately: ". . . I believe verily, had the calm Weather held, I should have brought away the whole Ship Piece by Piece" (pp. 56-57).

Crusoe's interest in the material world is clearly not merely utilitarian. While escaping from the Moors, he gratuitously shoots an enormous lion and is then "very sorry to lose three Charges of Powder and Shot upon a Creature that was good for nothing" (p. 28). He takes the skin, thinking it may be of some use. It is: he lies on it for a time, and the Portuguese captain later gives him forty ducats for it. But the use that Crusoe so vaguely apprehended is the excuse for the action, not its cause. Here too, Defoe's planning is no more rational than Crusoe's. The episode is not contrived to provide money or a bed for Crusoe: these are afterthoughts. When Crusoe's Moorish adventure is ended, everything is scrupulously transformed into the money needed for the next episode—boat, Xury, lion's skin, leopard's skin, bottles, guns, and beeswax (pp. 33-34). Nothing must be abandoned; Crusoe and Defoe share their attachment to things.

Among the memorable passages of *Robinson Crusoe* is the apostrophe to money: ". . . O Drug! . . . what art thou good for, Thou art not worth to me, no not the taking off of the Ground, one of those Knives is worth all this Heap, I have no Manner of use for thee, e'en remain where thou art, and go to the Bottom as a Creature whose Life is not worth saving" (p. 57). These words are resoundingly false: we are accustomed by this time to see a conflict between Crusoe's abstractions and his actions. Here this conflict is brought sharply to our attention by the contrasting matter-of-fact tone of the immediately succeeding reversal: "However, upon Second thoughts, I took it away, and wrapping all this in a Piece of Canvas, I began to think of making another Raft." But one does not have to conclude that Crusoe's materialism is being derided—only that he has two thoughts, both of which are justified.[7] He plausibly argues that "we enjoy just as much as we can use, and no more" (p. 129). Just as plausibly, he suggests that money might be hidden on the island and recovered if he escapes (p. 193).

Our confidence that he will not leave the money behind results in part from our faith in consistency of character. Crusoe is a collector—and not only of money. His emotions are controlled and defined by many kinds of objects. Surrounded by his booty, he is able to rest "very secure" as the storm breaks up the wreck (p. 57). With "infinite Labour" he carries things to his new habitation (p. 59): "... it was a great Pleasure to me to see all my Goods in such Order" (p. 69). He reluctantly thinks of moving when an earthquake threatens to bury him: "... but still when I look'd about and saw how

[7] This passage has occasioned differences of opinion. Ian Watt, *The Rise of the Novel* (Berkeley and Los Angeles, University of California Press, 1957) p. 119, responds to Coleridge's admiration of the passage by wondering if "the apparent irony [is not] merely the result of the extreme insouciance with which Defoe ... jerks himself back to his role as novelist, and hastens to tell us what he knows Crusoe, and indeed anyone else, would actually do in the circumstances." William H. Halewood, "Religion and Invention in *Robinson Crusoe*," *Essays in Criticism* 14 (1964), 350, finds that this passage "concentrates in a little space the central irony of the book and the defining irony of Crusoe's inconsistent character." If "irony" means only the recognition of a discrepancy between conduct and statement, temporarily unnoticed by a character, then this passage is ironic: surely both Defoe and his narrator, Crusoe, must be assumed to be aware of the sharply presented contradictions here. But if in a broader sense, it is meant that Defoe designed a structure to expose the failings of Crusoe's whole mode of behavior—failings never fully recognized by the character himself —then it seems to me that the passage is not ironic.

every thing was put in order, how pleasantly conceal'd I was, and how safe from Danger, it made me very loath to remove" (p. 82). Having his goods again reduced to a "confus'd Heap" (p. 67) is more distressing than the danger.

Crusoe's dogged collection of the unneeded corresponds to Defoe's cataloging of the irrelevant. Crusoe "got very little . . . that was of any use" (p. 193) from his voyage to the Spanish wreck; nevertheless what he got is listed in several hundreds of words. The enumerating, the organizing of oneself in verbal possessions, is the comfort, perhaps cold, of writer and character: the quantity of material collected by the one has its analogue in the language compiled by the other. The impulse to barricade oneself appears even in metaphor: "I was now come to the Center of my Travels, and had in a little Time all my new discover'd Estate safe about me" (p. 303). This estate is money, his new fortress. Defoe's contradictory claims, in the *Serious Reflections*, for the reality of his book are perhaps relevant here. He insisted on Crusoe's autonomy, on the historical authenticity of the book, but he would not give up the opposing claim that the book reflected his own life. It was his accretion, not Crusoe's.

The most directly expressed of Crusoe's emotions are his fear of being devoured and his hatred of the wild men and beasts who devour. There is for him a fate worse than death—subsequently being eaten up: his body is his last barricade. The cannibals who visit the island produce extravagances of fear and hatred in him—intensities of emotion that are sustained for years. After he first learns of the cannibals, he can think of nothing but how he "might destroy some of these Monsters in their cruel bloody Entertainment, and if possible, save the Victim they should bring hither to destroy" (p. 168; the emphasis of the sentence is signifi-

cant). He has fantasies and dreams of killing them: "...
sometimes that I was just going to let fly at them in
my Sleep" (p. 169). Both prudential and religious considerations restrain his murderous imagination for a
time, but after another visit from the savages he dreams
not only of killing them but also of how he "might justify
the doing of it" (p. 185). He finally decides that Friday
can be used to kill a group of cannibals from another
nation because he is in a state of war with them. But
seeing a white victim, Crusoe is "enrag'd to the highest
Degree" (p. 233). He prepares a balance sheet at the
end of the account to record the number of savages
killed (p. 237).

As Frank Ellis points out, the parts of the book before
and after the island adventure are filled with references
to creatures who eat people—the beasts and cannibals
of Africa and the bear and wolves of the Pyrenees.[8] But
some of these dangers of Africa (and the island) exist
only in Crusoe's imagination. He sails southward to
escape the Moors: "... for who would ha' suppos'd we
were sail'd on to the southward to the truly *Barbarian*
Coast, where whole Nations of Negroes were sure to
surround us with their Canoes, and destroy us; where
we could ne'er once go on shoar but we should be
devour'd by savage Beasts, or more merciless Savages
of human kind" (p. 23). Obviously Crusoe himself regards this as hyperbole, and in fact he encounters little
difficulty with savages or animals. Nevertheless the
"hideous Cryes and Howlings" of beasts and the fears
of Crusoe and Xury are frequently mentioned (pp.
24-25). And early in his island sojourn, Crusoe's principal
fear is of dangerous wild beasts, though there is never
any evidence of their existence. These fears are finally

---

[8] "Introduction," *Twentieth-Century Interpretations of Robinson
Crusoe,* ed. Ellis (Englewood Cliffs, N. J.: Prentice-Hall, 1969), pp.
12-13.

externalized in the encounter with the wolves of Languedoc: ". . . the Howling of Wolves run much in my Head; and indeed, except the Noise I once heard on the Shore of *Africa* . . . I never heard any thing that filled me with so much Horrour" (p. 297). These are "hellish Creatures" (p. 299), "three hundred Devils . . . roaring and open mouth'd to devour us" (p. 302).

The ubiquitous references to being devoured point to a generalized fear: of being dematerialized—the reversal of the desire to accumulate. It is a fear shared by author and character; "being devoured" is a way of conceiving of diverse fears. Even the language of a passage not directly concerned with cannibals or beasts suggests devouring. Before the shipwreck, Crusoe and the crew expect to be, and are, "swallowed up" (pp. 41, 44); they fear being saved from the sea but devoured by the cannibals (p. 42); the sea is "wild" (p. 43; attention is called to this word, "*Den Wild Zee*, as the *Dutch* call the Sea in a Storm"); the sea pursues Crusoe "as furious as an Enemy" (p. 44); and buries him "deep in its own Body" (p. 45).

The fear represented in the book is finally of the rage within. Knowing his own rage, Crusoe fears the worst of others. When his aggressive impulses are thwarted, he improves his fortress in fear of vicious enemies. When his overimproved habitation affords diminishing opportunities for elaboration, he discovers a cave that is suitable for defense. Frightened by an old goat in the cave, he reassures himself: ". . . I durst to believe there was nothing in this Cave that was more frightful than my self" (p. 177). Although Crusoe has been meditating "a bloody putting twenty or thirty of them to the Sword" (p. 169), he gives no sign of recognizing any ironic meaning in his statement. Crusoe's possessions and fortress, Defoe's lists and amplifications—all serve as self-protective psychic diversions.

Crusoe's expectations of violence are not, however, foundationless; much of *The Farther Adventures* is a documentation of ungovernable passion. The irrational violent impulses of the three mutineers left on the island are brought under control only after several battles with savages. The actions of Crusoe's men at what he calls the "massacre of Madagascar" (XIII, 102) are "Instances of a Rage altogether barbarous, and a Fury, something beyond what was human" (XIII, 96). When suspected of being a pirate, Crusoe will not surrender, even though he can prove his innocence; he agrees with his partner: ". . . we could have expected nothing from them, but what Rage would have dictated, and an ungoverned Passion have executed" (XIII, 122). Crusoe, finally repelled by the continual bloodshed, is pleased when the Cochin-Chinese (who howl like the wolves of Languedoc) are vanquished with the loss of only one life: ". . . for I was sick of killing such poor Savage Wretches, even tho' it was in my own Defence" (XIII, 129).

But his bloodlust is revived. Traveling through China, he indulges in indirect, then direct, insults to the natives. He is clearly bent on mischief even before he finds an idol to provide a focus for his rage. When he learns that a Russian who affronted the idol had been sacrificed, Crusoe "related the Story of our Men at *Madagascar*, and how they burnt and sack'd the Village there, and kill'd Man, Woman, and Child . . . I added, that I thought we ought to do so to this Village" (XIII, 184; Crusoe's previous expressions of abhorrence of this massacre had driven his men to mutiny). Restrained by the information that the sacrifice had occurred at another village, Crusoe organizes an attack on the idol. The subsequent destruction is an exhibition of wild rage exercised against a surrogate human (XIII, 188).

The moral character of this incident is ambiguous

in a way that is rare in *Robinson Crusoe*. It is not
unusual for an event to be left open to interpretation,
but Crusoe usually at least ponders its possible meanings. Rarely is there even a suspicion of Defoe looking
with irony on Crusoe's final perceptions. Here the reference to the Madagascar incident quite clearly puts
Crusoe in the wrong, but there is no more explicit
recognition of guilt. Indeed, Crusoe's behavior is in some
ways exemplary: he prevents the others from doing
serious harm to the villagers, and justifies his destructive
actions as a demonstration of the idol's falseness (the
Tartar's angry pursuit of Crusoe and his companions
shows that they have not learned the lesson that Crusoe
intended). And to vindicate Crusoe, one may also cite
"Of the Proportion Between the Christian and Pagan
World" from the *Serious Reflections*, where it is argued
that the Christian nations ought by force to eradicate
the worship of idols (p. 230).

Crusoe's action is explicitly justified and implicitly
condemned. The idol's appearance links it with the
earlier cannibals and devouring animals: it is a ludicrous
conglomeration of the features of various animals, wearing a garment and a hat (XIII, 180). Animals and, on
one occasion, a man are sacrificed to it; the priests
resemble butchers. Crusoe restrains his earlier rage
against the cannibals by religious arguments; here he
justifies identical feelings as religious zeal. These moral
ambiguities result from contradictory desires of the
author: to describe the frenzied mutilation of the idol
and also to bring Crusoe (and the book) to a stasis,
to a condition in which he is no longer at the mercy
of irrational drives.

The pattern for *The Life and Strange Surprizing
Adventures of Robinson Crusoe* is that of a fall, repentance, and redemption—both spiritual and secular. A
coincidence of dates, among other things, attests to this

pattern's providential order (p. 278): Crusoe's spiritual and physical welfare have been brought about by God's interventions. Within this structure are subsidiary narrative cycles (the island episode is the major one) that are interconnected by many cross-references. The ending, however, represents only temporary salvation. Crusoe's fortune is made, but he will continue the rambling that has been symptomatic of his evil. The obvious explanation is that Defoe is touting *The Farther Adventures*.

However, there is an additional reason for his continuing the book. The religious structure has not resolved the psychological problem: Crusoe's story has been organized according to a traditional pattern that does not explain his behavior. The continuation is consistent with the earlier book, but it turns out to be no more conclusive. *The Farther Adventures* sends Crusoe back to the island to tidy up left over narrative matters: the people remaining on the island are organized in a society, and their experiences are shown to be in some ways analogous to Crusoe's. Obsessions from the earlier work are repeated—eating and being eaten, massacres and fortifications. Nevertheless, the only larger order that Defoe finally imposes on the book is a physical one: Crusoe's rambling ceases when he encircles the globe.

In a sense, *The Farther Adventures* reflects Defoe's recognition of disharmonies in the earlier work. It represents the same impulses, but does not so effectively present the structures used to disguise and control them; aggressive impulses build up, are sated, and build up again. Defoe seems powerless to construct any other pattern. The hostility that drives the writer away from a "design" that he himself recognizes is evident in the following laughably overblown sentence—its very prolixity a testimony both to the writer's self-knowledge and his inability to restrain himself:

... and therefore, I must confess, it seem'd strange to me, when I came home, and heard our People say such fine Things of the Power, Riches, Glory, Magnificence, and Trade of the *Chinese*; because I saw, and knew, that they were a contemptible Herd or Crowd of ignorant sorded Slaves, subjected to a Government qualified only to rule such a People; and in a word, for I am now launch'd quite beside my Design, I say, in a word, were not its Distance inconceivably great from *Muscovy*, and was not the *Muscovite* Empire almost as rude, impotent, and ill govern'd a Crowd of Slaves as they, the *Czar* of *Muscovy* might with much Ease drive them all out of their Country, and conquer them in one Campaign; and had the Czar, who I since hear is a growing Prince, and begins to appear formidable in the World, fallen this Way, instead of attacking the Warlike *Swedes*, in which Attempt none of the Powers of *Europe* would have envy'd or interrupted him; he might by this time have been Emperor of China, instead of being beaten by the King of *Sweden at Narva*, when the latter was not One to Six in Number (XIII, 153).

Providence and original sin are the central conceptions that Crusoe uses to explain his earlier life. They are organizing patterns in the book and also essentials of Defoe's faith. But this tells us little about *Robinson Crusoe*—or Defoe. How do these beliefs affect Defoe's imagination? How are they used in *Robinson Crusoe*?

"Of Listening to the Voice of Providence," from the *Serious Reflections*, resolves a few questions. The essay asserts clearly and repeatedly a faith in "the supervising influence and the secret direction of the Creator"; it is man's duty to attempt to understand this secret direction (p. 179). But Defoe recognized enormous difficulties in discerning the dispositions of Providence. His essay is burdened with references to the propensities of men for "tacking the awful name of Providence to every fancy of their own" (p. 196).

In *Robinson Crusoe*, Providence often seems to be a method of interpretation, a theory rather than a force. And on several occasions, events suggest that it may be Crusoe's "fancy." He thinks that his impulse to go to the Spanish wreck "must come from some invisible Direction" (p. 189), but on returning he not only regards his trip as fruitless but also sees that it intensifies his discontent. His subsequent dream of saving a savage, is, he thinks, providential. But it is a response to his desire to have someone to help him escape to the mainland; this desire is "the fruit of a disturb'd Mind, an impatient Temper" (p. 198). When his dream seems to come true, he notes his less than complete reliance on it: ". . . I did not let my Dream come to pass in that Part, *viz*. That he came into my Grove for shelter" (p. 205).

Providence seems to be of two minds about Crusoe's rescue: it prepares him to escape with the aid of the Spaniards, and also sends an English ship. Before rescuing the Spaniard, Crusoe had "Testimonies of the Care of Providence" and an "invincible Impression" that his "Deliverance was at hand" (p. 229). After rescuing the Spaniard, he thinks that he is to be provided with a crew to sail away, a supposition that is supported by the increases in his grain: the supply he is raising for the journey increases tenfold, an allusion to the blessings in the parable of the sower (p. 247). But "a strange and unforseen Accident" occurs—an English ship arrives (p. 249). Crusoe later thinks of this event as evidence of the "secret Hand of Providence governing the World" (p. 273). Although he is not entirely unaware of the difficulties of understanding what he calls the "Checquer-Work" (p. 304) of Providence, this awareness rarely seems to inhibit his speculations.

An inexplicable Providence is of course an aid to Defoe's next book: Crusoe is unexpectedly taken off, the Spaniards and rascally Englishmen are left behind to provide further adventures. But the separation between author and character which is implied by these manipulations is not complete: Crusoe and Defoe continue to respond to forces not explained by their conceptions of Providence or of potboilers. Crusoe's aversion to going from Portugal to England by sea is providentially inspired, as he shows by his account of subsequent shipping disasters (p. 288). Nevertheless, he forgets about Providence after encountering wolves: ". . . I think I would much rather go a thousand Leagues by Sea, though I were sure to meet with a Storm once a Week" (p. 302).

In *The Farther Adventures*, Providence becomes psychological as well as theological. Crusoe has dreams of the evils committed by the Englishmen on his island: they are "never all of them true in Fact" but in general. This, he thinks, suggests the "Converse of Spirits" (XII, 113). Clearly, he feels guilty for deserting the Spaniards, although he previously attributed his leaving the island to Providence. He later acknowledges that even at the time of his rescue he feared what the rascally English mutineers who were left behind would do (XII, 148). The difficulty of applying his conception of Providence to his experience becomes apparent, and he despairs of rational comprehension of the meaning of his life. We are "hurry'd down the Stream of our own Desires" (XIII, 82); although it is our duty to listen to the voice of Providence, it is "impossible to make Mankind wise, but at their own Expence" (XIII, 102).

Original sin too becomes a psychological as well as a theological conception. Crusoe calls his leaving home to ramble his *"Original Sin"* (p. 194); he has no rational object in mind, but is powerless against the compulsion: "But my ill Fate push'd me on now with an Obstinacy that nothing could resist" (p. 14). His repentance subdues this impulse—but only partially and temporarily.

The language of disease and mental illness is used to describe Crusoe's condition at the beginning of *The Farther Adventures*—"chronical Distemper" (XII, 112); "Extasies of Vapours" (XII, 113); he tries to control himself by working on his farm. When his nephew proposes a voyage, Crusoe attributes the suggestion to the Devil (XII, 120), but then gives Providence the blame (XII, 121). Theological language is Crusoe's device for explaining his psychological instability. This time Defoe accepts the consequences of his creature's unregenerate nature and keeps him in motion. In the final sentence, the old and exhausted Crusoe is preparing "a longer Journey than all these" (XIII, 220). The metaphor is retained even in the face of death.

The Farther Adventures embodies Defoe's increased understanding of Crusoe; much that is only implicit in the earlier work is explicit in the later one. In particular, the limitations of Crusoe's repentance are clearly shown in *The Farther Adventures*. But the later book is less interesting than the earlier one. The incongruities between structural device and psychological reality provide an order for the first account. Crusoe's use of religious conceptions to subdue his destructive impulses is both limiting and useful: although his theories do not explain his experience, they enable him to order his responses. In *The Farther Adventures*, Crusoe's disordered impulses result in a distended narrative—obsession without form.

In the earlier work, Crusoe's repentance is narrated in a traditional literary structure—a journal. The awkwardness of Defoe's use of this structure is expressive of the complications of the book. The journal begins ordinarily enough as a day-to-day account of his experiences, but soon Crusoe interprets events from a later point of view. The departure from the journal is frequently unnoted, but when it becomes apparent, variations of the formula "But to return to my Journal" (p. 79) are used to wrench the narrative back to its former structure. Vestiges of the journal remain for some time, but the form is of little narrative use after Crusoe's repentance and recovery.

The traditional use of a journal among the religious was to find and memorialize the spiritual significance of daily existence. One expects this kind of account here because Crusoe begins with events already narrated: what purpose can there be if not to reveal a spiritual dimension? But at first, the journal account is no more spiritual, or even internal, than his previous account: in its compression, it is usually a balder summary of external activity than the first account. It affords in fact the same satisfactions as his earlier frenetic activity: the process of external ordering hides the disorder within. Earlier he briefly described the state of his affairs in writing: ". . . not so much to leave them to any that were to come after me, for I was like to have but few Heirs, as to deliver my Thoughts from daily poring upon them, and afflicting my Mind" (p. 65). Following this exercise, he is able to bring his possessions into order: he exerts a "prodigious deal of Time and Labour" (p. 68) just to make shelving for his goods. By then he has not only attained the stability necessary for keeping a journal but has also acquired a need for this new stabilizing enterprise. The first part of his journal allows the previous ordering process to be enjoyed again.

The providential appearance of the grain is the first substantial departure from the journal form. As Crusoe expatiates on Providence, he moves away from his point of view as a castaway: his consciousness at that time is corrected and expanded until it disappears. Following this, the journal structure is violated extensively: the ill and inactive Crusoe is terror-stricken, and the spiritual significance of his repentance is explained by commentary from a later point of view.

It is not to Crusoe's diminishing supply of ink alone that we must look for an understanding of the exploded journal structure. Defoe could not plausibly have had Crusoe define his own spiritual condition. On the island, Crusoe is characterized by his obsessive actions: he finds pretexts, not explanations, for his behavior. His definitions of his condition must be supplemented by explanation from the vague and distant future. But Defoe's introduction of the journal is expressive as well as awkward. The gap between Crusoe's behavior and his explanations becomes apparent as additional commentary must be inserted to make the narrative assume the shape of a traditional repentance story.

The island experience is another structural device that is effectively exploited by Crusoe and Defoe. Traditional associations are alluded to, but the allegory is discontinuous; the island is interpreted in incompatible ways: it is "my Reign, or my Captivity, which you please" (p. 137). For Crusoe, the island is a way of defining moods; for Defoe, it is a way to shape a story. The *"Island of Despair"* (p. 70) is the wilderness (p. 130) where Crusoe must undergo the suffering that will take him through repentance to the promised land. But he transforms the wilderness into the garden; the island itself becomes his deliverance. The contradictions in his own thoughts are clear to Crusoe: he must subdue his anguish at being cast away, but he should also hope for his deliverance (p. 113). As he explores the island, he becomes increasingly aware that it can be made into a promised land. His habitation becomes "natural" (p. 110).

Defoe mentions many biblical parallels—the prodigal son and Jonah, for example.[9] But any extended interpretation of the story in terms of a single pattern is perilous: patterns obviously alluded to are often just as obviously incongruous. When Crusoe leaves the island, he gives those who remain various seeds "and bad them be sure to sow and encrease them" (p. 277). This incident combines references to two of Christ's parables—that of the sower, often alluded to in *Robinson Crusoe*, and that of the talents, traditionally interpreted as an injunction to prepare for Christ's return. This analogy to divinity, though not strictly suitable to Crusoe, is pursued in *The Farther Adventures*. The Spaniards remain in their original habitation because they expect to "hear from their Governor again, meaning me" (XII, 172). When he returns, they accept his food "as Bread sent from Heaven; and what a reviving Cordial it was to their Spirits to taste it" (XIII, 6). Crusoe soon explains that he did not come to remove them but "to establish them there" (XIII, 7). Their response to this chilling news: ". . . I was a Father to them, and that having such a Correspondent as I was, in so remote a Part of the World, it would make them forget that they were left in a desolate Place" (XIII, 10).

The obvious incongruities resulting from presenting

[9] Edwin B. Benjamin, "Symbolic Elements in *Robinson Crusoe*," *PQ* 30 (1951), 206-211, shows the importance of many of the biblical allusions. J. Paul Hunter, *The Reluctant Pilgrim* (Baltimore: Johns Hopkins Press, 1966) provides information about the conventions of Puritan religious writings, and interprets *Robinson Crusoe* from this perspective. George A. Starr, *Defoe and Spiritual Autobiography* (Princeton: Princeton University Press, 1965) also deals with traditional religious patterns in *Robinson Crusoe*.

Crusoe as a type of Christ are soon apparent. Crusoe sees how far he is from "understanding the most essential Part of a Christian" (XIII, 23). And in retrospect he comments upon his unkind behavior: ". . . I pleased my self with being the patron of those People I placed there, and doing for them in a kind of haughty majestick Way, like an old Patriarchal Monarch" (XIII, 80). Christ is a role adopted by Crusoe but also sustained by Defoe (Defoe has things external to Crusoe also suggest that he is a savior). The role is soon abandoned, but the attitude is later revived. Speaking to a Russian prince, Crusoe boasts: ". . . never Tyrant, *for such I acknowledged myself to be,* was ever so universally beloved, and yet so horribly feared by his Subjects" (XIII, 200). Christ or tyrant—he can play one as easily as the other.

Robinson Crusoe is highly allusive; yet the references to things outside the book do not lead to expanded meanings: reverberations are quickly muffled. "I might well say, now indeed, That the latter End of *Job* was better than the Beginning" (p. 284), says Crusoe as he recovers his wealth. This comparison at first seems ironical; Job, unlike Crusoe, was a righteous man. Although Defoe understood well the implications of the biblical story, one can find no indications of irony within the text. The reference is used in its limited sense: only Crusoe's ending is expressed in terms of Job's. The broader meanings of both stories are ignored.

Sometimes the allusions are vague, even subliminal. Crusoe fancies himself "like one of the ancient Giants, which are said to live in Caves, and Holes, in the Rocks, where none could come at them" (p. 179). A Polyphemus who is in terror of being himself eaten? (Eric Berne states that "Crusoe's anxieties were based on the principle: 'He who eats shall be eaten.'"[10]) One thinks of

[10] "The Psychological Structure of Space with Some Remarks

Crusoe's often described position on top of his hill looking for cannibals with his perspective glass (monocular). And another example: Crusoe agrees with the Spaniard "about a Signal they should hang out at their Return, by which I should know them again, when they came back, at a Distance, before they came on Shore" (p. 249). The signal is in vain; Crusoe has gone. Has Theseus's father revenged himself? Crusoe has been punished for filial contempt; in this case, he makes his children suffer. Pursuit of these threads does not lead to a precise delimitation of meaning but to the labyrinth where text and author meet.

Defoe surrounds Crusoe with fragments of meaning; the bare character is chaotic energy. Crusoe is the forms he adopts only for so long as he adopts them: his ultimate reality resembles that of Swift's Aeolists. Crusoe clothes himself in his accretions. What is within is formless and frightening; therefore he creates, in the terms of the clothes philosophy of *A Tale of a Tub*, an outer soul (*A Tale*, Section ii). Material accumulations, literary traditions, and traditional theology—all serve a self-protective purpose. He attempts to organize everything external as part of himself. But by his doing so, his enemy becomes both internal and external. He must attack any forces threatening the order that he uses to control his own feared impulses. What he desires is related to what he fears: the external is his defense and his enemy. He encloses himself in masses of material, and is afraid of being devoured.

Crusoe carefully constructs an appearance and critically scrutinizes it: he trims his whiskers like a Turk (p. 150); notes that his "Figure indeed was very fierce" (p. 253); and cannot "abide the thoughts" of going naked (p. 134). Friday too must be carefully dressed, even to a cap "fashionable enough" (p. 208). Crusoe externalizes whenever possible; the naked inside is native—and he must not go "native." Friday's name is a day in Crusoe's life, and Crusoe is a role—"Master" (p. 206).

Defoe and his creature are collaborators; they make a self-made man. Crusoe jests himself into a throne: "It would have made a Stoick smile to have seen ... my Majesty the Prince and Lord of the whole Island" (p. 149). His words make him "Generalissimo" (p. 267), and he later acts "for Reasons of State" (p. 268). This character who so fears the imagination is its creature and at its mercy. "I imagin'd ... I imagin'd ... I imagin'd" (pp. 186-187) pulsates through his narrative of the Spanish shipwreck: ". . . perhaps they might this Time think of starving, and of being in a Condition to eat one another" (p. 187).

Crusoe expresses confidence in a felicity beyond "human Enjoyments," but gives us only a record of fruitless motion:

> I saw the World busy round me, one Part labouring for Bread, and the other Part squandring in vile Excesses or empty Pleasures, equally miserable, because the End they propos'd still fled from them; for the Man of pleasure every day surfeited of his Vice, and heaped up Work for Sorrow and Repentance; and the Men of Labour spent their Strength in daily Strugglings for Bread to maintain the vital Strength they labour'd with, so living in a daily Circulation of Sorrow, living but to work, and working but to live, as if daily Bread were the only End of wearisome Life, and a wearisome Life the only Occasion of daily Bread (XII, 117-118).

It is not surprising that Samuel Johnson took great pleasure in *Robinson Crusoe*.[11] The man who was ap-

---

[11] "Was there ever yet any thing written by mere man that was wished longer by its readers, excepting Don Quixote, Robinson

palled by "that hunger of imagination which preys incessantly upon life, and must always be appeased by some employment"[12] found a book that expressed his insight but masked its bitterness. Crusoe is an overachiever; his activity has results that can be entered on a balance sheet. But when he looks to a higher order for approval, his accomplishments themselves are the only evidence of the existence of that other order. He is the victim of an unacknowledged solipsism.[13] Needing sympathy, he teaches Poll to say "Poor Robin Crusoe," and later starts up in "utmost consternation" at the unexpected words (p. 142).

A passage in Swift's *Tale of a Tub* describes both the structure of Robinson Crusoe and the central figure's mind:

> And, whereas the mind of Man, when he gives the Spur and Bridle to his Thoughts, doth never stop, but naturally sallies out into both extreams of High and Low, of Good and Evil; His first Flight of Fancy, commonly transports Him to Idea's of what is most Perfect, finished, and exalted; till having soared out of his own Reach and Sight, not well perceiving how near the Frontiers of Height and Depth, border upon each other; With the same Course and Wing, he falls down plum into the lowest Bottom of Things; like one who travels the *East* into the *West*; or like a strait Line drawn by its own Length into a Circle (Section viii).

Crusoe, and the Pilgrim's Progress?" *Johnsonian Miscellanies*, ed. George Birkbeck Hill (New York: Barnes and Noble, 1966), 1:372. It seems unlikely that Johnson had availed himself of the opportunity of reading *The Farther Adventures*.

[12] *Rasselas*, chap. 32.

[13] For a related discussion, see the section entitled "Boredom" in Thomas S. Schrock, "Considering Crusoe: Part II," *Interpretation: A Journal of Political Philosophy* (Winter, 1970), 211-216.

Crusoe's bathos derives from his metaphysical expansiveness, his attempts to soar; his flights toward the exalted end not just in a disappointingly ordinary reality but in "the lowest Bottom of Things." When he searches beyond everyday reality, he hopes to find the spiritual, the "Perfect, finished, and exalted." But his attempts to get out of himself betray what is within: rage, despair, disorder. Defoe successfully expresses Crusoe's bafflement but not alternatives to it. There is no greater structure into which Crusoe is absorbed: instead of an efficacious repentance, we are shown unremitting activity. *Robinson Crusoe* purports to move toward redemption, but it is "a strait Line drawn by its own Length into a Circle." Much space is traversed, but we end where we began.

Alvin Kernan shows that it is typical of satire to reflect these self-defeating movements;[14] yet *Robinson Crusoe* is not satiric. Swift loathed those who exemplified the condition that he described: in Swift's view, their aberrations were willful. But Crusoe is unwillingly mired in a materialistic world; he at least tries to organize his life as if it were a providential progress toward spiritual truth. That his progress, instead, may be a "Flight of Fancy" is a disappointment not finally admitted, or perhaps not fully recognized, by either Crusoe or Defoe. Defoe is no more distant from the Crusoe who acts than is the Crusoe who narrates; both share a sympathy for the creature of their story as well as a limited insight into his failure. Defoe drew a powerful—and, on occasion, poignant—portrait of the kind of figure who is the butt of much of the satire of Swift and Pope.

[14] *The Plot of Satire* (New Haven: Yale University Press, 1965), pp. 102-103.

III

Captain Singleton:
Puritan and Picaresque

The Life, Adventures, and Pyracies of the Famous Captain Singleton was published in 1720, the year after *Robinson Crusoe* and two years before *Moll Flanders*, *A Journal of the Plague Year*, and *Colonel Jack*. It may be unjustly neglected, but it is no masterpiece. Too much of the book remains mere material—accounts of travel, piracy, and business which are neither very interesting in themselves nor closely related to the development of character and moral vision. However, *Captain Singleton*'s failures call attention to some of the tensions in Defoe's other fiction. This book is a soggy amalgam of the picaresque and Puritan—two persistent strands in Defoe's writing.

Arthur Secord has argued that Defoe's fundamental methods of narration "are not derived from the picaresque tradition."[1] He is of course attempting to find specific sources for incidents in Defoe's works. When one considers Defoe's fiction less narrowly, the picaresque tradition seems highly relevant to it. In his study *The Picaresque Novel*, Stuart Miller defines the composite picaresque hero as follows:

> The hero of the picaresque novel differs from characters in other types of fiction. His origins are uncertain. He becomes a rogue in a world full of

[1] *Studies in the Narrative Method of Defoe* (New York: Russell and Russell, 1963), p. 230.

roguery. His roguery differs from comic roguery in being gratuitous. He cannot love or feel strong emotion; he is incapable of anchoring his personality to some idea or ideal of conduct. His internal chaos is externally reflected in his protean roles. This instability of personality is seen in the picaresque novel as a reflection of the outer chaos discovered by the plot patterns. The picaresque character is not merely a rogue, and his chaos of personality is greater than any purely moral choas. It reflects a total lack of structure in the world, not merely a lack of ethical or social structure.[2]

Miller's definition fits significant aspects of the lives of many of Defoe's heroes, although it does not exactly describe any one of them.

Captain Singleton, Moll Flanders, Colonel Jack, and Robinson Crusoe have much in common with the traditional picaresque hero. Singleton, Moll, and Jack have the usual picaresque beginnings, and they become the requisite rogues in a world of roguery. At first, Crusoe's alliance to his society is too close to fit the picaresque pattern, but as he circles the globe in *The Farther Adventures*, he becomes an outsider. All Defoe's major characters are protean: role playing is one of their common activities. But finally these characters do not develop in the direction of the picaresque. They draw back from their sense of outer and inner chaos, and attempt to impose an order on their world. They persist in attaching themselves to "some idea or ideal of conduct," however dubious it may be.

[2] *The Picaresque Novel* (Cleveland: Case Western Reserve University Press, 1967), p. 131. Miller discusses the following novels: *Lazarillo de Tormes* (1554), *Guzmán de Alfarache* (1559 and 1605), *The Unfortunate Traveller* (1594), *El Buscón* (1626), *Simplicissimus* (1668), *Gil Blas* (1715, 1724, 1735), *Moll Flanders* (1722), and *Roderick Random* (1748).

The young Singleton clearly resembles the picaro that Miller describes. But after years of piracy, he repents. Defoe's moral didacticism is not necessarily inconsistent with the traditions of the picaresque: Alexander A. Parker has shown that the Spanish prototypes of the picaresque novel are imbued with a moral perspective condemning the actions of the picaro.[3] But there is an inevitable strain in such novels: evil deeds must seem interesting as well as reprehensible. If a careful balance is not maintained, either the morality or the action will seem perfunctory. The Spanish writers of the picaresque sometimes resolved the problem by having the hero exiled from his normal world: after having lived part of his life with gusto, the picaro is withdrawn from worldly affairs, thus validating the moral perspective of his book. The hero of Alemán's *Guzmán de Alfarache* undergoes a conversion after being sentenced to the galleys, and the hero of Quevedo's *El Buscón* goes to the Indies, where his life is even worse than it was at home. Later writers of picaresque novels severely restrict their moral judgments on their heroes. The picaro survives as best he can, and in his hard world few moral principles can seriously be applied to his actions. Smollett's Roderick Random, for example, is partially excused because of the wickedness of his world. But Defoe will not abandon the broader moral issues raised by his picaros, nor will he have them renounce this world in favor of the next: he is Protestant, and his characters must work out their salvation here. But when these characters remain prosperous through wickedness and through penitence, they sometimes seem to have attained only respectability, not salvation. We feel that the pleasures leading to hell have enabled them to gain

[3] *Literature and the Delinquent: The Picaresque Novel in Spain and Europe,* 1599-1723 (Edinburgh: Edinburgh University Press, 1967), pp. 1-74.

the rewards of heaven. Instead of evil giving way to good, we may sense honesty giving way to hypocrisy, either in Defoe or in his characters.

Defoe's problem in making his heroes' repentances plausible is related to his Puritanism.[4] The Puritan cannot abandon the world: he must observe God's world in order to discover His will. Also, it is man's duty to build an earthly city in harmony with the heavenly one. These religious conceptions are of course much older than Puritanism. But for the eighteenth-century dissenter, they presented a special problem and acquired a peculiar character. Without the sanctions of a Church established by the state, the dissenter attempted to thrive in a society that, at least in theory, he rejected. He had the obvious difficulty of distinguishing between God and Caesar, a problem that is apparent in the island episode of *Robinson Crusoe*: the island is "The Island of Despair," a wilderness that Crusoe must traverse to find his redemption, but Crusoe turns it into a remarkably pleasant land.

In Puritan literature as well as in picaresque fiction, the alliance of the spiritual and the secular is an uneasy one. Bunyan solved the problem at the expense of the secular. *The Pilgrim's Progress* is a dream, and the world exists almost exclusively for its emblematic significance. When Bunyan deals more concretely with the problems of this world in *Grace Abounding*, his salvation occurs only after much grief, and it brings no secular reward. Even the wickedness that he recounts is so petty that

[4] Stuart Miller, *The Picaresque Novel*, dismisses Defoe's Puritanism as Defoe's attempt to placate his audience (pp. 118-119, 121-122). He finds *Moll Flanders* to be essentially picaresque; the moralism of the book is for the purpose of getting it "past the objections of the Puritans" (p. 119). However, Defoe's heroes are only intermittently picaros. Much of what is most interesting in Defoe is derived not merely from the picaresque elements in his books but from the collusion (or collision) of the Puritan and the picaresque.

it gives neither him nor us much pleasure. When Bunyan describes a more accomplished sinner in *The Life and Death of Mr. Badman*, he makes it clear from the very beginning that Badman is damned. But Defoe and Richardson emphasize secular experience, although, in addition, suggesting its emblematic significance. The traditional relationship between the spiritual and the secular sometimes seems to be inverted in these writers, the spiritual becoming only an adjunct to secular success.

Perhaps the salient example of this equivocal relationship of the spiritual and the secular is *Pamela*. Pamela is put into a fully described material setting. That her virtue is rewarded within this setting has been enough to damage the book for many readers, among them Fielding. To these readers, Pamela's virtue is merely an attitude that she strikes in order to achieve material ends. The only thing that can convince the reader of Pamela's integrity is his sense of her inner world. But even if we feel that both Pamela and Richardson are hypocritical, the book remains interesting so long as we are convinced that Pamela's hypocrisy is believable and significant. The reality that we look for is psychological, not spiritual.

Defoe's is an analogous case. His works are not damaged by the religious attitudes that he expresses in them, even if we feel that these attitudes are in themselves hypocritical. The flaw is in the incongruity that results when he has his characters express attitudes that we feel are inappropriate to them. The character, we feel, may be a hypocrite, but not in the way that Defoe suggests. Defoe's use of picaresque patterns exacerbates his difficulties in convincing his reader of the psychological validity of his characters. The nearest thing to an excuse for the picaro is the evil of his world; consequently there is a consistency in the picaro's repenting and renouncing his world. And one can also easily imagine the picaro unrepentantly preying on society from the inside as he once did from the outside (it is less dangerous and more profitable). But Defoe asks us to believe that his picaros have both repented and become part of their wicked world.

This incongruity is least damaging when the hero's wickedness is not blatant. For example, in the first part of *Robinson Crusoe*, the central figure's failures are insisted upon, but he is not egregiously evil. Crusoe's main link with the picaro is in his wandering, his becoming an outsider who rejects the ties of family and country and neglects his religion. At the end of the first part of *Robinson Crusoe*, we can believe that Crusoe's rather coarse mind does not find his repentance incompatible with his materialism. He is not a perceptive man, but his impercipience is of interest. Captain Singleton is, however, implicated in open evil throughout much of his life. The facts of his life so obviously contradict his final pretensions that he cannot possibly fail to see his own egregious hypocrisy. That Defoe earlier shows him developing a moral consciousness makes the ending seem especially false. This book, unlike *Robinson Crusoe*, does not convince us of the psychological validity of its central character.

Defoe's fiction often all too clearly has a beginning, a middle, and an end: the connections are sometimes missing, and the various parts of the central character's experience seem unrelated. This weakness is often found in plots taking the form of a journey, but it is not inherent in them: character and theme often do provide unity. Captain Singleton, however, seems to be several different characters—in childhood, on Madagascar, in Africa, as a pirate, as a merchant, as a penitent. There are interconnections, but emphases change to fit demands external to his character. He lacks integrity. But

Defoe's failures and successes are often related. For example, much of the interest of *Robinson Crusoe* is aroused by Crusoe's attempts to find a pattern in his life. He adopts various roles to allay the anxiety resulting from his sense of incoherence.

One of Defoe's major achievements in his prose fiction is his creation of this version of the hollow man—a character who, because of his sense of inner vacuousness or incoherence, desperately tries to give a shape to his life through conventional piety and the rituals of business. Of course Defoe himself sometimes seems not to grasp the incongruities of his character's actions: he is not always the calculating author. For example, he is obviously hesitant to disturb Crusoe's comfortable equilibrium at the end of the first part of *Robinson Crusoe*; he is implicated in his creature's coarseness. But in *The Farther Adventures*, he shows that he recognizes some of the implications of Crusoe's life. Throughout his prose fiction, Defoe attempts repeatedly and in varied ways to give a form to this kind of character. This persistence suggests that he well understood at least the central issue of his fiction—the tenuous relationship between a surface of bourgeois respectability and the chaos within.

It is true that *Captain Singleton* appeals to the rather trivial interests of Defoe's audience: exploration and the lives of buccaneers. But a comparison of *Captain Singleton* with its source, *The King of Pirates*, reveals that in *Captain Singleton* Defoe attempted seriously to impose form and significance on his earlier narrative.

The King of Pirates purports to be the pirate Avery's attempt to set straight the falsely sensational accounts of his life. Avery acknowledges a sense of wrongdoing, but in general he defends himself. Moral issues are subdued: the pirates are presented merely as one kind of community among others. The account occasionally touches on Avery's personality, but the emphasis is on the putative facts of the pirates' lives. Avery eliminates what is merely personal: "I shall not trouble my friends with anything of my original and first introduction into the world. . . ."[5] Much of this earlier work is used in *Captain Singleton*, but the emphasis has shifted. Singleton's early life is recounted in detail, and his piracy is dealt with in less limited moral terms.

The one element of psychological interest in *The King of Pirates*—the pirates' desire to go home—is made the thematic center of *Captain Singleton*. After Avery and his pirates are rich and comfortable on Madagascar, they, and especially Avery, wish to go home, despite the obvious dangers. Avery finally goes to Marseilles, "from whence I intend to go and live in some inland town, where, as they perhaps have no notion of the sea, so they will not be inquisitive after us" (p. 90). Avery's story, despite its superficial modesty, is implicitly a glorification of his life as a pirate; nevertheless he abandons everything (except his money) so that he can live obscurely in Europe. The naming of the hero of Defoe's subsequent version of this story is significant. Defoe first systematically shows how Singleton is separated socially and morally from any normal human community. The remainder of the book deals with his uneasy return to England and its values.

The opening pages of *Captain Singleton* evoke the normal human bearings only to show the hero's alienation from them. He comments ironically on his "Pedigree," about which he has only second-hand information (p. 1).[6] He evokes the horror that he thinks (hopes?) his parents must have felt when he was stolen from

<hr/>

[5] *The King of Pirates*, ed. George Aitken (London: J. M. Dent, 1895), p. 7. Subsequent references are to this edition.

[6] All references are to the Oxford English Novels edition, ed. Shiv K. Kumar (London: Oxford University Press, 1969).

them, but he concludes by saying "it would make but a needless Digression to talk of it here" (p. 2). He is "disposed of" to various people who can use him, and is told that his name is Bob Singleton, "not *Robert*, but plain *Bob*; for it seems they never knew by what Name I was Christen'd" (p. 2). A kind master of a ship takes him from his town, "whatever its Name was" (p. 3); Singleton "would have called him Father, but he would not allow it, for he had Children of his own" (p. 3).

Singleton is separated from all communities. Captured by Turks and recaptured by Portuguese, he is unmoved. But "my Master, who was the only Friend I had in the World, died at *Lisbon* of his Wounds; and I being then almost reduced to my primitive State, *viz*, of Starving, had this Addition to it, that it was in a foreign Country too, where I knew no body, and could not speak a Word of their Language" (pp. 3-4). When he demands wages of his next master, the stingy man wrongfully calls him heretic: "Indeed of all the Names the Four and Twenty Letters could make up, he should not have called me Heretick; for as I knew nothing about Religion, neither *Protestant* from *Papist,* or either of them from a *Mahometan,* I could never be a Heretick" (pp. 7-8). His master swears that Singleton is a Turk, and the boy realizes that he can prove nothing about himself. He is finally cleared by what has not been done to him; he is uncircumcised (pp. 8-9). Involved in a mutiny and expecting to be hanged, he does not "remember any great Concern ... for I knew little then of this world, and nothing at all of the next" (p. 10). He can identify himself with nothing external, not person, country, or religion.

In retrospect, the narrator has found an identity for himself—the picaro. In tone and content, this account

of Singleton's early life resembles *Lazarillo de Tormes*.[7]
The tone is hard-boiled and contemptuous, exploiting
the comic possibilities of the boy's ignorance more than
the pathetic. He is partially excused for his own rascality
by the much greater villainy of those around him, but
he learns their arts rapidly and enthusiastically: "Fate
certainly thus directed my Beginning, knowing that I
had Work which I had to do in the World, which nothing
but one hardened against all Sense of Honesty or Religion could go thro' " (pp. 6-7). The narrator comments
ironically that a priest made him "as good a *Papist* as
any of them in about a Week's Time" (p. 8). Fortunately
for Singleton, he does not learn so fast as he wants to;
having decided to poison his master, he cannot find any
poison (p. 9).

The narrator believes that Providence frustrated his
murderous designs, but he does not know for whose
sake—his or his master's (p. 9). He conceives of this past
self as a malignant nonentity. "I kept no Journal," he
reiterates (pp. 3, 9). This statement defines the distance
between the mature writer and the boy: it alludes to
the pious duty of recording one's experience to discern
its pattern. Although the narrator is doing just that,
his contemptuous references to this younger version of
himself suggest his doubts that any spiritual order
extends to someone like him at that time.

An identity is later forged out of the unpromising
materials of Singleton's indifference to most human and
supernatural ties. He is efficient because he is not
subject to metaphysically induced hesitations:

> This thoughtless, unconcern'd Temper had one
> Felicity indeed in it; that it made me daring and

[7] Secord, *Studies in the Narrative Method of Defoe*, p. 163, notes
the resemblance.

ready for doing any Mischief ... whereas my Companions in the Misery, were so sunk by their Fear
and Grief, that they abandoned themselves to the
Misery of their Condition, and gave over all
Thought but of their perishing and starving, being
devoured by wild Beasts, murthered and perhaps
eaten by *Cannibals, and the like* (p. 12).

When the others want to go home, Singleton is unconcerned: "... I was on no Side, it was not one Farthing
Matter to me, I told them, whether we went or stayed,
I had no home, and all the World was alike to me"
(p. 35). But, on the whole, he does prefer Madagascar,
because he forsees the possibility of becoming rich by
piracy.

Money humanizes Captain Singleton; it introduces
him to those frivolous, metaphysical, even spiritual
values that are irrelevant to survival. He violates an
agreement by keeping money that he had stolen, instead
of putting it into the common fund: "... and none of
them ever suspected that I had any more Money in
the World, having been known to be only a poor Boy
taken up in Charity, as you have heard, and used like
a Slave" (p. 20). Money is useless here, but Singleton
obviously enjoys feeling superior to the other sailors'
conception of him. He does not hesitate to break agree-
ments, but he has at least the rudimentary ties of vanity
and greed to bring him into an organized society.

On the journey across Africa, Singleton's elementary
sense of self develops into a clearer conception of his
relations with others. He takes more responsibility for
leading the group (p. 54); he begins to think of himself
as English, as superior to the Portuguese (p. 55); he
develops "an insatiable Thirst after Learning in general"
(p. 56). He was affected by a "religious Thought" for
the first time in his life—gratitude that he was not born

a savage (p. 61). His assumption seems inaccurate, but it does reflect his developing conception of himself. As they approach the "vast howling Wilderness," he is "as much affected with the Sight as any of them," the first time that he has shared his companions' trepidation (p. 79).

Captain Singleton is episodic and cyclic, but also progressive. After Singleton's initial deracination, he acquires an identity and returns to England a rich man. He then loses his money, becomes a pirate, and returns to Madagascar, again apart from all normal societies. His final return to England ends the book, but in each cycle there is also a progression: the condition to which Singleton reverts is in some respect a change from the previous cycle.

On his first return to England, he foolishly spends his money on people who are not his friends: "... I conceived a just Abhorrence of their Ingratitude; but it wore off; nor had I with it any Regret at the wasting so glorious a Sum of Money, as I brought to *England* with me" (p. 138). Neither greed nor the elementary moral conception of gratitude is firmly enough established in him to make him share the values of English society. He boards a ship, and agrees to mutiny, "... for I did not care where I went, having nothing to lose, and no Body to leave behind me" (p. 138). He and his companions set out to prey upon the Spaniards, but end by attacking all ships indiscriminately (p. 141). The captain, Wilmot, apparently murders all captured Englishmen, and the narrator decides to "bury [this part] in Silence for the present" (p. 142). They finally arrive at Singleton's "old Acquaintance the Isle of *Madagascar*" (p. 171).

Geographically and morally, Singleton seems to have reverted to an earlier stage of development. But there are differences. There is in the book a sense of an impending wicked destiny but also, as in *Robinson Crusoe*, a sense of liberation in fulfilling it: "I that was, as I have hinted before, an original Thief, and a Pyrate even by Inclination before, was now in my Element, and never undertook any Thing in my Life with more particular Satisfaction" (p. 140). Significantly, Singleton and Harris, the man who organized the mutiny, "called one another Brothers," the first such familial relationship that Singleton has had since he was forbidden to give his kind master the name of "Father" (p. 138). Also in his career as pirate, Singleton develops the virtue of forbearance; the occasional unruly malevolence of his earlier days seems almost entirely subdued by his sense of practicality. When threatened by Avery and Wilmot, he responds with circumspect kindness (p. 185); and he avoids fighting whenever possible (p. 190).

Singleton is finally a bourgeois pirate. His piracy is just good business, and he is like any other crafty merchant. A major problem in piracy is disposing of goods, and on one occasion the pirates trade with merchants whom they have just robbed (p. 199). When the pirates want revenge for an attack by natives, William the Quaker, who is Singleton's adviser, reminds them, ". . . if I mistake not, your Business is Money" (p. 219). He argues that it would be murder to kill the natives "as much . . . as to meet a Man on the High-way, and kill him, for the mere sake of it" (p. 219). One assumes that if a profit is involved, the moral is changed.

William—a Quaker, pirate, and moralist—sums up the contraries of the book. He is committed to systematic hypocrisy, and bare legality is enough to satisfy any of his moral impulses. Wishing to accompany the pirates, he has them give him a certificate that he was taken forcibly (p. 143). When he gives the pirates advice, as he often does, he will do so only indirectly. He often lies, but whenever possible he is technically truthful.

The narrator comments with ironic amazement after William tells one of his "plausible" tales, which deceives without deviating from the truth: ". . . *William* past for what he was; I mean, for a very honest Fellow" (p. 165). Appearance and reality have for William equal value: he keeps them in conflict, thus being all things to all men. He has no particular respect even for the appearance of Quaker which he so assiduously cultivates. When Singleton is about to lose a ship that William is greedy to capture, the Quaker gibes, "I am greatly in hopes, Friend . . . Thou wilt turn Quaker, for I see thou art not for Fighting" (p. 148).

William's practical attitude influences Singleton and the other pirates: he prevents many actions that are motivated by unthinking bloodlust. But having this rascally Quaker suggest repentance to Singleton compromises the moral tone of the ending—against Defoe's wishes, one assumes. It is difficult to believe in any integrity in William, especially when he decides that now is "the fairest Occasion" for repentance (p. 259). He acts only when the moral coincides with the practical; he and Singleton are then rich and in a good situation to escape from their comrades.

William is one of the few minor characters often mentioned by writers about Defoe: ". . . one of the most memorable creations in Defoe's fiction."[8] Certainly he is one of the most totally corrupted. Rarely does he do anything out of emotion; he is, consequently, saved from some evils and from unprofitable good. He is not plagued by a longing for an identity; he is Proteus. He has no unfulfilled romantic longings to be one with his world; his world is various, and so is he. There is no inhibiting continuity to his life and, consequently, no sense of discontinuity. The only unity to his character is his grave, although witty, language and his rationality.

[8] Kumar, *Captain Singleton*, p. xiv.

He is the only developed character in Defoe's works who is perfectly adapted to his world. Sin, respectability, and repentance—all come easy to him. But of course such a character cannot be the central one; he evades the problems that trouble Defoe.

William is used to define Singleton's difficulties and progress. In one incident, savages have attacked the crew and seem to have an impregnable position in a large tree: "Never was a Fortification so well defended, or Assailants so many ways defeated; we were now for giving it over, and particularly I called *William*, and told him, I could not but laugh to see us spinning out our Time here for nothing. . ." (pp. 212-213). On this occasion, William, somewhat inconsistently, insists on revenge, and the Gunner finally blows up the hideout: ". . . there we saw what was become of the Garrison of *Indians* too, who had given us all this Trouble; for some of them had no Arms, some no Legs, some no Head, some lay half buried in the Rubbish of the Mine. . ." (pp. 213-214). It is Singleton who responds to the incident with the practical wisdom that might be taken for humanitarianism.[9] He is learning with difficulty to perform the feat that William usually accomplishes with ease—manipulating a moral code for practical purposes without ever being inexpediently moved by it.

But Singleton never quite achieves William's moral

[9] Manuel Schonhorn, "A Reassessment of Defoe's *Captain Singleton*," *PLL* 7 (1971), 49, comments that Defoe's heroes avoid "physical aggression and ritual action," both of which "demand an intimacy on the personal and social level of which Defoe's protagonist are incapable." One might add that Defoe's heroes are often eager observers and describers of scenes of violence and lust from which they dissociate themselves. Crusoe raptly observes the cannibals whom he hates, and also, like Singleton, he describes scenes of violence in such detail that one perceives his relish of them.

suavity. Singleton's life presents problems that threaten even William's assurance. William suggests abandoning piracy when they are rich, "for no body trades for the sake of Trading, much less do any Men rob for the sake of Thieving" (p. 256). To this easy rationalist certainty, William adds his next assumption: "... it is natural for most Men that are abroad to desire to come Home again at least, especially when they are grown rich" (p. 256). William is "quite stunn'd" (p. 257) at Singleton's response: "Why, Man, I am at Home" (p. 256). When asked if he has any relations or friends in England, Singleton replies, "... no more than I have in the Court of the Great *Mogul*" (p. 257).

Singleton senses his own metaphysical vacuity, but he does not have the traditional comfortable alliances that other men use to placate spiritual needs. Disconcerted, William goes beyond what he first intended to suggest—retirement—and instead proposes repentance (p. 258). What he intends is a gradual abandoning of the past, physically and morally, until all is obscured by distance. But Singleton's sense of himself differs from William's; it disturbs Singleton to abandon the identity that he found with such difficulty. He dreams that the Devil asks him his name and trade. Singleton answers: "... I am a Thief, a Rogue, by my Calling; I am a Pirate, and a Murtherer" (p. 269).

Of William, Singleton says, "... he was my Ghostly Father, or Confessor, and he was all the Comfort I had" (p. 268). William has facile answers for Singleton which are based again on the coincidence of the practical with the moral. "But what then must be done with our Wealth, *said I*, the Effects of Plunder and Rapine" (p. 266); William answers, "... we ought to keep it carefully together, with a Resolution to do what Right with it we are able" (p. 267). Singleton determines to kill himself: "... I could not support the Weight and Terror that was upon me" (p. 268). William responds with his usual rationality: the next life will be worse for Singleton (p. 268). William's religion is of this world. He is a good pirate, and his search for Christianity leads to the via media: he and Singleton become merchants.

The subject of the final section is more accurately described as disguise than as repentance. To mislead their pirate associates, they write a letter, falsely stating that they have been betrayed (pp. 262-263). Immediately Singleton feels guilt; no longer a pirate, his destiny, he must become something. They dress "after the *Persian* Manner," but Singleton's sense of inauthenticity makes him mock the disguise: ". . . we could not understand or speak one Word of the Language of *Persia*, or indeed of any other but *English* and *Dutch*, and of the latter I understood very little" (p. 264). Eventually they get enough "of the *Persian* and *Armenian* Jargon . . . as was sufficient to make us able to talk to one another, so as not to be understood by any Body, though sometimes hardly by our selves" (p. 272). They converse "upon the Subject of . . . Repentance continually; we never changed . . . so as to leave off our *Armenian* Garbs, and we were called at *Venice* the two *Grecians*" (p. 272). Simulating a new identity severs them from the old one. The peace that passeth understanding comes from a perfect disguise.

Vast expanses of time and space are evoked throughout the book. Singleton believes that the pirates' ship is grounded where no ship ever was before (p. 220). One of his final voyages is "monstrous" (p. 204). Perhaps he and William have more money than was "brought into the City by Two single Men, since the State of *Venice* had a Being" (p. 272) But despite all these references, the world of the book is claustrophobic. These vast expanses are barely enough for Singleton to escape his evil. He must travel the world in order to settle anonymously in a little village, to insinuate himself discreetly into a small family.

The ending is domestic. Repentance is essential, but only routine. More important, Singleton must be made into what he never was before—a family man. William's widowed sister, sensing that her brother and Singleton wish to be hidden, finds a house outside London (p. 275). Singleton consents to return to England only after she has accepted money from him and he is convinced that her gratitude will not permit her to betray him. Of course he finally marries her.

But the conditions that Singleton makes for his return to England show the limits of this new social role:

> Why first, *says I*, you shall not disclose your self to any of your Relations in *England*, but your Sister, no not to one.
>
> Secondly, we will not shave off our Mustachoes or Beards, (for we had all along worn our Beards after the *Grecian* Manner) nor leave off our long Vests, that we may pass for *Grecians* and Foreigners.
>
> Thirdly, That we shall never speak *English* in publick before any body, your Sister excepted.
>
> Fourthly, That we will always live together, and pass for Brothers (p. 277).

Singleton acknowledges that he is elaborating a disguise, not finding an identity.

Alienation in Defoe's works must not be confused with *Weltschmerz*. Throughout much of their lives, characters such as Singleton are in danger of violent death. They may be legally executed or murdered by their fellow criminals. When they think of spiritual matters, they conceive of them in terms of final retribution. All the symptoms of the more genteelly alienated are theirs, but in addition they have nightmares that are close to reality.

The distance between Defoe's fiction and his life is not so great as the extravagance of his plots might suggest. His fictional representations of fear and disguise have their analogues in his biography.[10] Although his life was of course markedly safer than Singleton's or Moll's, both his undercover work for various governments and his private life frequently put him into an ambiguous, even dangerous, relationship with his society. The possible penalties for aberrant behavior in Defoe's time were stringent. For most readers of eighteenth-century literature, the pillory and ear cropping are jests in Swift and Pope. But reality gave the jests a flavor then that they now lack. Defoe was lauded after standing in the pillory, but when sentenced to it he had no reason not to believe that he might be maimed by an angry crowd. He was probably in danger of the pillory repeatedly. On one occasion, his employer Mist was pilloried for an article that Defoe repudiated. A sense of alienation was induced in a man in Defoe's position not only by metaphysical causes but also by the possibility that his mutilation and murder might be socially sanctioned. The nature of societal relationships is a central concern of Defoe and his characters.

In Defoe's works, the relationships between repentance and reintegration into society is close and ambiguous. Sometimes the social and the spiritual seem identical. Robinson Crusoe must become a castaway in order to repent; yet when he gets back to England, presumably repentant, the spiritual concerns that he acquired on

[10] See James Sutherland, *Defoe*, and John Robert Moore, *Daniel Defoe: Citizen of the Modern World* (Chicago: University of Chicago Press, 1958), for many relevant biographical details, among them the accounts of Defoe and Monmouth's rebellion, bankruptcy, the pillory, service with Harley, and writing for Mist.

his island seem to disappear. Sometimes the conditions of the alienated sinner's return to society are so morally compromised that the repentance itself seems insignificant. Moll Flanders finds a place in society after her repentance, but she still evidences many of the traits and some of the money that she acquired in her life of crime.

Captain Singleton deals with the social concerns related to repentance far more than with repentance itself. A prodigious blast of lightning, in Puritan literature a sign calling men to repentance, has no lasting effect, but the men "fell a calling for one another, every one for his Friend, or for those he had most Respect for; and it was a singular Satisfaction to find that no body was hurt" (p. 196). In the wastes of Africa, Singleton and his companions are continually in battle against beasts. They are at pains to assert themselves as a human community, even in their construction of relatively temporary shelters:

> Our Camp was like a little Town, in which our Hutts were in the Center, having one large one in the Center of them also, into which all our particular Lodgings opened; so that none of us went into our Apartments, but thro' a publick Tent where we all eat and drank together, and kept our Councils and Society, and our Carpenters made us Tables, Benches, and Stools in Abundance, as many as we could make use of (p. 98).

The digression on Knox late in the book helps to clarify the focus of *Captain Singleton*. Knox is the example by which to measure others. Detained on Ceylon, he maintains his religion and his desire to return home. The digression is apologetically introduced as a warning of the dangers from the Ceylonese: ". . . I think it cannot but be very profitable to record the other

Story, *which is but short*, with my own, to show, whoever reads this, what it was I avoided, and prevent their falling into the like, if they have to do with the perfidious People of Ceylon" (p. 238). This simpleminded justification is clearly aimed only at simple readers. Knox's narrative presents straightforwardly the issues that the book has been dealing with ambiguously: the moral symbolism of money and of the return to England.

Knox's prosperity is from God: "... God so prospered him, that he had Plenty, not only for himself, but to lend others; which being according to the Custom of the Country, at 50 *per Cent.* a Year, much enriched him" (p. 243). To us Knox's usury may seem to be next to piracy, but Defoe leaves no moral ambiguities in this account. Knox's desire to return to his home is evidence that he is a good man: "... he could not so far forget his native Country, as to be contented to dwell in a strange Land where there was to him a Famine of God's Word and Sacraments, the Want of which made all other things to be of little Value to him" (p. 243). In this account, Defoe associates money, religion, and the social world of England. Money cannot be enjoyed without religion, and religion is best enjoyed in England. Each of these elements is most satisfying if joined to the other two.

For Singleton and his renegade friends, the search for wealth is sometimes corrupting but at other times evidence of a morally desirable attitude. When gold is readily available in Africa, the sailors are only with difficulty persuaded to postpone their journey home. Unlike Knox, they do not have a strong sense of a social world larger than their immediate one. This deficiency prevents them from valuing wealth properly. A strong social sense would make greed a virtue and lead to godliness; an assiduous search for gold in Africa should be followed by reintegration into a godly community in England. Singleton's neglect of his fortune in Africa is evidence of his debasement; going home is not in itself good:

> ... none of the rest had any Mind to stay, nor I neither, I must confess; for I had no Notion of a great deal of Money, or what to do with my self, or what to do with it if I had it. I thought I had enough already, and all the Thoughts I had about disposing of it, if I came to *Europe*, was only how to spend it as fast as I could, buy me some Clothes, and go to Sea again to be a Drudge for more (p. 132).

His lack of "Regret at the wasting so glorious a Sum of Money" after he returns to England is evidence of Singleton's continued hardness of heart (p. 138). Yet when he finally returns to England with a great deal of money, it is of little value to him because he is deprived of a society to give it meaning. He is then condemned to keep it:

> ... though I had money in Profusion, yet I was perfectly destitute of a Friend in the World to have the least Obligation or Assistance from, or knew not either where to dispose or trust any Thing I had while I lived, or whom to give it to, if I died (p. 176).

Defoe's fiction often associates wealth and salvation, but, whatever his intention, wealth leads to richer lives for his characters only in the literal sense. The depressing futility of their search for wealth makes salvation too seem trivial. After their necessities have been met, the accumulating becomes meaningless, except as evidence of their, and Defoe's, obsessions. The ritualistic recounting of wealth only makes more obvious how unsatisfying it is. If the mess of pottage signifies the blessing, the blessing itself is not alluring.

Defoe was conscious of the fascination of money, but he was also conscious of the tawdriness of human economic arrangements. His analysis of the African trading in *Captain Singleton* is a mordant comment on the more complicated but similar European society. Money is of no value to the natives, but an animal made of a coin "not worth Six-pence to us ... was worth an Hundred Times its real Value" (p. 28). The "artificer" in Singleton's party obtains great quantities of gold for little figures made of baser metals (p. 136). The repeated references to the "artificer" emphasize the element of fraud in art and business: by playing on savage weaknesses, this man makes the surface more valuable than the substance. Singleton sees this economic pattern as evidence of the "Folly of the poor People" (p. 28). But the trading of more common goods connects the priates' activities in Africa with ordinary business procedures: "... for Ten or Twelve Pound Weight of smoked dry'd Beef, they would give us a whole Bullock, or Cow" (pp. 38-39). In this context, Singleton's piracy is not so great a departure from business as it first seems.

Defoe has difficulties distinguishing between pirate and businessman in *Captain Singleton*. Nevertheless, he does believe that there is a difference, even if some businessmen are piratical. He is not writing a *Beggar's Opera*.[11] Moral distinctions are continually being made, even if the various moneymaking schemes do tend to shade into each other. Yet Defoe's distinctions are often

[11] Maximillian Novak, *Economics and the Fiction of Daniel Defoe* (Berkeley and Los Angeles: University of California Press, 1962), p. 103, suggests that Defoe's writings on pirates should be read with the analogy in mind that Gay develops in *The Beggar's Opera*—that between thieves and respectable members of society. This is an illuminating analogy, but Defoe does not intend it quite so literally as Gay presents it in *The Beggar's Opera*.

arbitrary: what he knows does not always seem compatible with what he believes.

Singleton's repentance seems to be merely a conclusion arbitrarily imposed on the book. In a world in which good and evil are so closely related, repentance becomes only a disjunction of oneself and one's past, followed by a future not radically different. How can an ending, fictional form, be imposed on such a life? Given these conditions, a sense of finality can be conveyed only in secular terms. Often in Defoe, the ending is even a diminished version of the secular—the geographical. Crusoe encircles the globe, and Singleton returns to England.

Defoe attempts to give the journey through Africa spiritual implications by using traditional biblical allusions. Gary Scrimgeour, in his study of the sources of the African adventure, states that much of the description is composed of stock details from many other accounts. He concludes that the sense of realism in Defoe's narrative is damaged by the thinness of detail: Defoe omitted much that was assumed to be true about Africa.[12] However, Defoe was not primarily concerned with the realism of the travel book. He was attempting to extend the dimensions of the account to what we now call the archetypal and what the Puritan called the typical. Defoe's narrative suggests the journey of the Israelites from Egypt to the Promised Land, a pattern used symbolically in many Puritan narratives to imply man's passage from his sinful origins to his final redemption. Like the Israelites, Singleton's company finds salt water in the desert. Like Moses, the surgeon promises the disappointed men to "make that salt Water fresh" (p. 111). Singleton wonders by what

[12] "The Problem of Realism in Defoe's *Captain Singleton*," *HLQ* 27 (1963), 27-28.

"Witchcraft" he will do so. The surgeon's sand filter is no miracle, but the parallel is clear.

In general, Defoe places this experience in a vast temporal and spatial context, having implications that are not sharply localized. Singleton believes that they are the first to set foot in this place "since the Sons of *Noah* spread themselves over the Face of the whole Earth" (p. 105). And even the ubiquitous references to elephants reinforce the sense of enlarged dimensions, not only in bulk and number but also in time—their skulls do not decay in the vast boneyards (p. 87).

The beasts that Singleton's group meets are frightening but only dimly apprehended antagonists: "... we could not see them; but their was a Noise and Yelling, and Howling, and all sort of such Wilderness Musick on every Side of us, as if all the Beasts of the Desart were assembled to devour us" (p. 90). The only snake that they meet is openly symbolic: "... an ugly, venemous, deformed kind of a Snake or Serpent ... it had a hellish, ugly, deformed Look and Voice, and our Men would not be perswaded but it was the Devil, only that we did not know what Business Satan could have there, where there were no People" (p. 105). The pious reader could of course supply morals not apparent to the pirates.

However, seeing the journey in specifically religious terms complicates rather than clarifies. The future is England, where Singleton loses his money. The mountain views in Africa are reminiscent of Pisgah (pp. 111-112, 133), but in the distance they see the desert of the past, not the Promised Land: "... the Prospect was indeed astonishing; for as far as the Eye could look, South, or West, or North-West, there was nothing to be seen but a vast howling Wilderness, with neither Tree or River, or any green thing" (p. 112). That desolate prospect is their future as well as their past.

Whatever Defoe's intentions, the religious overtones seem to emphasize the sleaziness of life instead of its providential order. For example, Providence appears to lead Singleton's party to rescue an Englishman held by savages: "Heaven by some Miracle that never was to be expected, had acted for him" (p. 121). He is the one who helps them to find the gold that makes this their "happy Journey" (p. 136). Later he "died ... of Grief; for having sent a Thousand Pound Sterling over to *England* ... the Ship was taken by the *French*, and the Effects all lost" (p. 137).

Defoe repeatedly tries to move his story into a realm of less tawdry and more spiritual implication. The captain's decision to maroon the mutinous seamen on Madagascar turns into a debate between Mercy and Justice (pp. 15-18); he finally allows them to have tools and weapons, "that they might not perish" (p. 18). But the story soon settles down to the dogged but not heroic efforts required for survival. Years later, when the cruel Captain Wilmot decides to leave Madagascar, "... nothing could perswade him, but he would go into the *Red Sea* with the Sloop, and where the Children of *Israel* past through the Sea dryshod, and landing there, would travel to *Grand Cairo* by Land" (p. 183). The implied contrast of this reprobate to the chosen people is so little needed as to appear gratuitous. Defoe alludes to classical mythology even more vaguely: Singleton and his companions are told when to leave Madagascar by "an Old Man who was blind, and led about by a Boy" (p. 35).

These allusions do not expand into patterns of great significance. The narrative persists in collapsing into banalities. Piracy becomes a branch of trade, and exploration a problem in transportation. Defoe professes to eliminate matters that are either uninteresting or insignificant, but without apology he organizes the trip across Africa as a succession of methods of transportation. Each stage of the journey is punctuated by a discussion of the new traveling arrangements. We are given details about lightening canoes, making knapsacks, and dividing the load. One of the minor triumphs of the trip is the discovery that the added burden of tent poles can be transformed into an easier way to carry baggage (p. 84). The appeal is not even to an interst in adventure but in the mechanics of adventure.

Here, as in *Robinson Crusoe*, Defoe shares some of the failures of his narrator: Singleton's concern for banalities is also Defoe's. But the significant failure in *Captain Singleton* is Defoe's too arbitrary imposition of an ending on unresolved conflicts and incongruous materials. The first part of *Robinson Crusoe* is successful because the narrator has an illuminating misapprehension of his life: his attempt to order incongruities brings them within the compass of a single character. But Captain Singleton has committed himself to denying his past. He is telling us his story of course, but with little comprehension of it except as several blocks of narrative material. He is several characters, a problem that Defoe discerns. In *Moll Flanders*, Defoe solves this problem by suggesting a more comprehensive view than the narrator's. But in attributing complete understanding to Singleton, he merely makes the contradictions more obvious. Instead of ordering the disparities of the book, Defoe fragments his narrator.

IV

Moll Flanders:
Parodies of Respectability

Robinson Crusoe and *Captain Singleton* have double perspectives, those of the narrator and of the person he once was. In these books, Defoe simulates a character's attempts to organize his own past. But because Defoe's narrators are enmeshed in their own history, their accounts of the past must inevitably be limited or implausible. In *Moll Flanders*, Defoe attempts to measure the impercipience of his narrator. He tries to show the full moral of his fable by developing a third perspective, intermittent but discernible.[1]

[1] In recent years, *Moll Flanders* has received a great deal of attention. Rather than list the many works that have been relevant to my understanding of the novel, I have chosen to call the reader's attention only to a relatively few statements about the major issues in the book. A useful survey of the debate about irony in *Moll Flanders* is Ian Watt, "The Recent Critical Fortunes of *Moll Flanders*," *ECS* 1 (1967), 109-126. In addition, three articles published after Watt's survey are of unusual interest: Douglas Brooks, "*Moll Flanders*: An Interpretation," *EIC* 19 (1969), 46-59; Maximillian E. Novak "Defoe's 'Indifferent Monitor': The Complexity of *Moll Flanders*," *ECS* 3 (1970), 351-365; William J. Krier, "A Courtesy Which Grants Integrity: A Literal Reading of *Moll Flanders*," *ELH* 38 (1971), 397-410. Douglas Brooks has included an expanded version of his article on *Moll Flanders* in his *Number and Pattern in the Eighteenth-Century Novel* (London: Routledge and Kegan Paul, 1973). In his book, Brooks also deals with *Robinson Crusoe*, *Captain Singleton*, *Colonel Jack*, and *Roxana*. He shows that there are many recurring patterns in these novels, and he relates these recurrences to Defoe's use of a numerological tradition.

Defoe's preface is not merely a justification for a salacious book but also a guide to the reader. While insisting on the authenticity of Moll's memoirs, the preface calls attention to editorial interventions. Although the story is Moll's, the language and moralizing are in part the editor's: "In a Word, as the whole Relation is carefully garbl'd of all the Levity, and Looseness that was in it: So it is all applied, and with the utmost care to vertuous and religious Uses."[2] Furthermore, the preface implicitly warns the reader against accepting Moll's perspective:

> The Pen employ'd in finishing her Story, and making it what you now see it to be, has had no little difficulty to put it into a Dress fit to be seen, and to make it speak Language fit to be read: When a Woman debauch'd from her Youth, nay, even being the Off-spring of Debauchery and Vice, comes to give an Account of all her vicious Practises, and even to descend to the particular Occasions and Circumstances, by which she first became wicked, and of all the progression of Crime which she run through in threescore Year, an Author must be hard put to it to wrap it up so clean, as not to give room, especially for vitious Readers to turn it to his Disadvantage (p. 1).

Defoe prepares the reader to understand more than Moll does: her view is the partially debased one that resulted from her life. She is repentant, but the effects of her wicked life have not mysteriously disappeared by the time that she writes the book.

Captain Singleton, like Moll, ostensibly organizes his story to explain his spiritual life. At the end, he can presumably understand his past wickedness with the

[2] *Moll Flanders*, ed. George Starr (New York: Oxford University Press, 1971), p. 3. All references to *Moll Flanders* are to this edition.

acuity of an uncorrupted man. But the material, and some of the psychological, accumulations of the past remain: he is rich and evasive. Defoe explains how Singleton becomes a certain kind of man, but he also relies on Singleton to point out the broader implications of his own life. Unfortunately, the man that Singleton became could not plausibly have understood what Defoe made him say. Unlike Singleton, Moll is not entrusted with the full meaning of her story.

The opening passages of *Moll Flanders* specifically identify her as a criminal whose crimes have gone unpunished. She could not give her real name even if a general pardon were issued (p. 7). In substance, there is nothing in this that is different from *Captain Singleton*: it is clear from the title pages of both books that they are about criminals. But Singleton comments on his early life without explicitly identifying himself as a criminal. In contrast, Moll Flanders emphasizes her mature identity even as she describes her early innocent life. Defoe's concern for establishing a limited point of view is shown also by numerous clumsy explanations of Moll's sources of information (for example, p. 17); "as I heard afterwards" (p. 131) is a recurrent afterthought.

The early episodes show the forming of Moll's consciousness.[3] As a little girl, she needs money to stay with her "Nurse," her surrogate mother. Later, people who are charmed by her give her coins. When her first lover offers guineas for sex, her erotic pleasures confirm the association of gold with love. But when her lover offers her money to abandon him, the symbolism must

[3] Many studies concentrate heavily, if not exclusively, on this opening section. Two important ones are these: Robert R. Columbus, "Conscious Artistry in *Moll Flanders*," *SEL* 3 (1963), 415-432; Juliet McMaster, "The Equation of Love and Money in *Moll Flanders*," *Studies in the Novel* 2 (1970), 131-144.

be revised. She rejects love, and determines to find her pleasure in money.

By the end of the opening segment of *Moll Flanders*, the Colchester episode, Moll's values have undergone the transformation that both protects and corrupts her. Her new attitudes resemble those of the coarse but practical narrator: "The Case was alter'd with me, I had Money in my Pocket, and had nothing to say to them: I had been trick'd once by *that Cheat call'd* LOVE, but the Game was over; I was resolv'd now to be Married, or Nothing, and to be well Married, or not at all" (p. 60). The narrator sees this as a downward step without recognizing its residual force in her present consciousness. The young Moll's deliberate choice is now a part of the narrator's sensibility.

Subtly and precisely, Defoe commingles the hard voice of the old Moll and her passionate younger self:

In short, if he had known me, and how easy the Trifle he aim'd at, was to be had, he would have troubled his Head no farther, but have given me four or five Guineas, and have lain with me the next time he had come at me; and if I had known his Thoughts, and how hard he thought I would be to be gain'd, I might have made my own Terms with him; and if I had not Capitulated for an immediate Marriage, I might for a Maintenance till Marriage, and might have had what I would; for he was already Rich to Excess, besides what he had in Expectation; but I seem'd wholly to have abandoned all such Thoughts as these, and was taken up Onely with Pride of my Beauty, and of being belov'd by such a gentleman; as for the Gold I spent whole Hours in looking upon it; I told the Guineas over and over a thousand times a Day: Never poor vain Creature was so wrapt up with every part of the Story, as I was, not Considering what was before

me, and how near my Ruin was at the Door; indeed
I think, I rather wish'd for that Ruin, than studyed
to avoid it (pp. 25-26).

The young girl is ruining herself, as the narrator suggests, but it is to her credit that she "seem'd wholly
to have abandoned all such Thoughts" as those that
the narrator is thinking. The narrator sees and continues
to share her former infatuation with money, but the
complexities of her former sexual nature escape her. The
young Moll is sexually excited by the money; the narrator's avarice is aroused by the sex.

The young girl's feelings are suppressed with difficulty. She becomes distraught and ill when abandoned
by her lover, and she retains her sexual feelings for him,
even after marrying his brother: ". . . I committed Adultery and Incest with him every Day in my Desires"
(p. 59). As the narrator tells of these events, she com-
municates the interest that the lurid aspects of her past
still hold for her, but she is impatient with the nuances
of her past feelings. Indeed, those feelings that are
unsubordinated to a utilitarian purpose are precisely
what the narrator finds most contemptible about her
younger self.

The entire Colchester episode has an emphasis differing from the narrator's. Of the moment that she loses
her virginity, the narrator comments: ". . . thus I finish'd
my own Destruction at once, for from this Day, being
forsaken of my Vertue, and my Modesty, I had nothing
of Value left to recommend me, either to God's Blessing,
or Man's Assistance" (p. 29). She ignores all the complexities of her story in order to emphasize this conventional judgment. But the more crucial moral event for
the young girl is a later one—her marriage to Robin.
The account of Moll's relationship to the elder brother
suggests that she is not willfully evil but naive and
sexually excited. She believes that she is as effectually

married to the elder brother "as if we had been publickly Wedded by the Parson of the Parish" (p. 39). This private betrothal does not excuse her sexual misbehavior, but it does make her subsequent marriage to Robin a greater evil than sex with his elder brother.

Both the young girl's interpretation of the story and the narrator's are distorted. The young girl concludes that she has been cheated by love: the narrator believes that she has managed everything wrong. The moral conception embodied in the episode is a combination of the perceptions of the narrator and of her younger self: practical wisdom and moral insight must not be severed; one must manage shrewdly in order to deliver oneself from evil. When Moll chooses to deny love for the sake of expedience, she severs her practical from her moral and emotional energies. She never fully recovers. The woman who tells the story sees her tactical errors, but she has little conception of what she might have been had she not made them. She thinks vaguely that she might have been better or richer, but she has no comprehension of the impoverishment of her sensibilities.

Conjugal Lewdness; or, Matrimonial Whoredom, Defoe's somewhat overheated and underlit "Treatise concerning the Use and Abuse of the Marriage Bed," discusses at length some of the domestic problems that are the substance of much of *Moll Flanders*.[4] To apply any expository work by Defoe to his fiction is risky. Defoe wrote with a well-developed sense of audience, and he argued to win; consequently his ideas are easily distorted when extracted from their context. And given that *Conjugal Lewdness* was published in 1727, five years after *Moll Flanders,* one must be cautious about

[4] References are to the facsimile reproduction introduced by Maximillian E. Novak (Gainesville, Fla.: Scholar's Facsimiles and Reprints, 1967).

using the treatise as if it were a plan for the novel. But the works are closely related in subject, and writing *Moll Flanders* was one of the experiences that shaped the author of *Conjugal Lewdness*.

In *Conjugal Lewdness*, Defoe describes marriage as potentially the best or worst condition in life: it is either the "Center to which all the lesser Delights of life tend, as a Point in the Circle" or a "kind of Hell in miniature" (*C. L.*, pp. 96, 103). Love is "that one essential and absolutely necessary part of the Composition ... without which the matrimonial State is, I think, hardly lawful, I am sure is not rational, and, I think, can never be happy" (*C. L.*, p. 28). Defoe returns to this theme throughout the treatise; the perversions of marriage are all related to the absence of love. Defoe particularly condemns marriages that are made primarily for economic or sexual reasons.

Defoe's heaviest emphasis in *Conjugal Lewdness* is on abuses of matrimony which are either sexually motivated or manifested. Presumably he is not attacking all sexual activity, but only sex divorced from its legitimating accompaniments—love, marriage, and childbearing (contraception is a conjugal lewdness). Marriage for primarily sexual reasons is "sheltering our Wickedness under the Letter of the Law" (*C. L.*, p. 267).

The treatise is aptly introduced by the couplets of the title page:

Loose Thoughts, at first, like subterranean Fires,
Burn inward, smothering, with unchaste Desires;
But getting Vent, to Rage and Fury turn,
Burst in Volcanoes, and like Aetna burn;
The Heat increases as the Flames aspire,
And turns the solid Hills to liquid Fire.
So, sensual Flames, when raging in the Soul,
First vitiate all the Parts, then fire the Whole;

Burn up the Bright, the Beauteous, the Sublime,
And turn our lawful Pleasures into Crime.

Defoe's effort is to discover and suppress hidden lewdness where others may not even look for it—in marriage or in the motives for marrying. Anything that will lend itself to a sexual interpretation is assumed by Defoe to be sexual, if not exclusively, then primarily. Why do widows and widowers remarry precipitately? Why do people marry after the age of childbearing? The answer is almost invariable: "... the Effect of a raging, ungoverned Appetite, a furious immodest Gust of Sensuality, a Flame of immoderate Desires" (*C. L.*, pp. 341-342).

Defoe's Freudianism is almost orthodox, although hardly subtle. Sex is everywhere, and the fundamental moral imperative is that it somehow be controlled. Indulged, it is debilitating; repressed, it is disrupting. In pursuit of the sexual, Defoe interprets a dream impeccably. A widow who wishes to marry a much younger man is chided by a relative. The widow answers: "I can't live thus ... I am frighted to Death ... ever since Sir *William* died almost, I have been disturbed in my Sleep, either with Apparitions or Dreams" (*C. L.*, p. 234). Sir William appears to her on some nights, but at other times she sees "Another Shape; 'tis Sir *William*, I think, in another Dress" (*C. L.*, p. 234). Sir William does not speak, "but the other Appearance spoke to me, and frighted me to Death: Why, he asked me, to let him come to bed to me; And, I thought, he offered to open the Bed, which waked me, and I was e'en dead with the Fright" (*C. L.*, p. 234). The lady's relative understands that the problem is not with the supernatural: "Upon the whole, her Cousin found what Devil it was haunted her Ladyship; so she confessed, at last, that the Lady had good reasons for marrying; but then she argued warmly against her taking the young Fellow"

(*C. L.*, p. 235). But only a young man will do for this Lady, and she subsequently suffers for her self-indulgence.

To Defoe, sex is a constant dangerous pressure, and anything that does not oppose it is in its service. In *Conjugal Lewdness*, Defoe sanctifies the more repressive, even if trivial, social conventions; he finds that deviations from the norm are almost invariably sexually motivated. Some "Customs" are in themselves indecent and must be resisted, and it is always criminal to violate any custom in the direction of greater sexual freedom, even if the freedom is legal (*C. L.*, p. 339). The mere appearance of evil is a real evil: "Though every Indecency is not equally criminal, yet every Thing scandalous and offensive is really Criminal" (*C. L.*, p. 338).

The intemperate sexualistic morality of *Conjugal Lewdness* in some respects resembles that of the old Moll Flanders, who often condemns her sexual deviations without making any reasonable discriminations; like Defoe, she has enormous respect for convention. But Moll often indulges also in pleasant memories of the past, sometimes excusing obvious evil (although not usually sexual evil). In Defoe's terms, she is "committing the Crime again in the Mind, by thinking it over with Delight" (*C. L.*, p. 334).

The rigoristic tone of *Conjugal Lewdness* contrasts with that of *Moll Flanders*; the novel implies at least a small margin for human error. In *Conjugal Lewdness*, Defoe is defining evil that he believes often goes unrecognized. For this reason, he makes little attempt to establish gradations of evil, or to provide excuses for it. Nevertheless, it is possible to derive from the treatise a set of moral assumptions broad enough to apply to the larger world of *Moll Flanders*. Defoe does occasionally write with unusual sympathy of woman's restricted position in society. When a man's mistreatment of his wife causes her to loathe him, "she must have an uncommon Stock of Virtue, and be more a Christian than he ought to expect of her, if she does not single out some other Object of her Affection" (*C. L.*, p. 19).

Conjugal Lewdness deals directly with the issue of sexual experience after a betrothal but before marriage. As might be expected, all restrictions apply: the promise of marriage is binding and sex forbidden. A wife is a property, and any breach of civil restrictions is a moral fault: ". . . the Form [ceremony] gives the legal possession" (*C. L.*, p. 278). Premarital sex is also forbidden because of what it evidences: ". . . a wicked filthy ungovernable Inclination, that could not contain your self from a woman for a few Days" (*C. L.*, p. 281). But in such cases, Defoe places more blame on the man than on a woman who has not been forewarned: ". . . many (till then) innocent women, have been imposed upon by them [men] and ruined" (*C. L.*, p. 288). In *Conjugal Lewdness*, as in *Moll Flanders*, it is a greater evil than simple fornication for a woman to "marry one man and be in love with another . . . a Matrimonial Whoredom . . . one of the worst kinds of it too' (*C. L.*, p. 181).

The code of conduct that Defoe recommends in *Conjugal Lewdness* is higher than nature or law—it conforms, he feels, to Christian virtue. Nature is not by itself sufficient for the Christian: nature teaches the "Propagation of the Kind . . . but does it without regard to the limitations imposed by Heaven" (*C. L.*, p. 60). Anything sexual that is unnatural or illegal is obviously wrong, but Defoe reiterates his hope that he need not deal extensively with these grosser evils. Custom, however, sometimes betrays men into "such Liberties which the Savages and undirected Part of Mankind, do not take" (*C. L.*, p. 306). But there is no excuse for such violations of nature: "To be ignorant of a thing that Nature dictates, is shutting the Eyes against natural

Light ... so that the Ignorance is really as criminal as the Action" (*C. L.*, p. 313).

Moll Flanders deals with these grosser moral issues that Defoe does not wish to emphasize in *Conjugal Lewdness*. Moll retains a crude sense of the natural throughout her career: she avoids incest, and prefers not to wear men's clothes. But she loses the moral inhibitions that would raise her above mere nature, and eventually she is not even moved by the simple social ties that one would expect of "Savages." She does at first have a limited sense of what is right, although she is not motivated by religion. She has no "great Scruples of Conscience," but she "could not think of being a whore to one Brother, and a Wife to the other" (p. 31). She sacrifices this instinctive sense of rightness to expedience, and afterward increasingly suppresses her natural responses. In Newgate she uses religion as a structure for her regeneration, but before she can achieve the social standards of a Christian she must achieve the more primitive ones of nature. After her repentance, Moll would still be subject to some harsh strictures in the context of *Conjugal Lewdness*—but that the more rigorous parts of this treatise might even be appropriately applied to her is in itself evidence of her moral improvement.

The episodes of *Moll Flanders* are carefully, even rigidly, organized to illustrate the loosening of Moll's moral inhibitions and social ties. She first loves a man, although unmarried to him. She then reluctantly marries his brother, although pained at being separated from her lover. She next marries a tradesman for his gentlemanly appearance; she has a pleasant time with him, but parts from him with little feeling except annoyance at his poor management of money. Her developing hostility toward men then motivates her to trick an arrogant man into marriage with her friend. She then chooses a husband for herself because he has money and is good-tempered; he will not abuse her when he discovers that he has been tricked (p. 80). But he turns out to be her brother, and she loathes him: "... I could almost as willingly have embrac'd a Dog, as have let him offer any thing of that kind to me, for which Reason I could not bear the thoughts of coming between the Sheets with him" (p. 98).

Her next liaison is at Bath. She is now neither married nor planning to be faithful: "... knowing the World as I had done, and that such kind of things do not often last long, I took care to lay up as much Money as I could for a wet Day, as I call'd it" (p. 118). But Moll miscalculates in thinking that her sexuality is completely subordinated to material ends: "... the Inclination was not to be resisted ... I was oblig'd to yield up all even before he ask'd it" (p. 119). Moll feels that sex for pleasure is more shameful than sex for money, but Defoe's structure modifies her evaluation. Her still having "inclination" reveals that she has not yet suppressed every instinct of nature. She has fallen far in Defoe's terms, but she has further to go.

Her next relationships are intertwined. She keeps the bank clerk in ignorant abeyance while she marries Jemy the highwayman. When Jemy proves to be impoverished, she deserts him. Her narrowing conception of prudence is no longer subverted by untrustworthy feelings, even though Jemy is the first man that she has loved since the elder brother: "... I really lov'd him most tenderly" (p. 155), but "never broke my Resolution, which was not to let him ever know my true Name" (p. 159). She makes it impossible for him to interfere in her future life, and keeps him from using her money. After having Jemy's child, she marries the bank clerk.

Her marriage to the clerk is described as the only extended tranquility that she has experienced since her

youth. But the calmly economic terms that she uses
to explain her happiness (p. 189) suggest that this man
satisfies her only because she has deliberately restricted
her feelings. Moll believes that her rejection of Jemy
was wise; nevertheless, her feelings for him survive.
Although Moll never again responds to anyone without
having her feelings compromised by greed, she later
experiences a resurgence of love for Jemy.

Each episode marks how far Moll has fallen, and in
addition, further erodes some remaining scruple. Having
repressed her feelings for Jemy in order to achieve a
secure life, she is prepared to steal when the clerk dies.
Moll's first theft is one of the most intense experiences
of her life, comparable to her loss of the elder brother.
She passes into another circle of her hell, which has
Newgate at its bottom: "... I was under such dreadful
Impressions of Fear, and in such Terror of Mind, tho'
I was perfectly safe, that I cannot express the manner
of it" (p. 192).

But Moll cannot even be part of the community of
thieves; her fellow criminals soon become her gravest
danger. Repeatedly she is saved because others are not.
She gets the "joyful News" that an accomplice is hanged
(p. 220). She is "easie" because all witnesses against her
are hanged or transported (p. 223). She is hated by other
criminals because she always escapes when they are
"catch'd and hurried to Newgate" (p. 214). The "Court"
too separates Moll from other criminals: it will pardon
anyone who gives the testimony that will hang Moll
(pp. 222-223).

As Moll's morality disintegrates, she clutches more
desperately at respectability. She adapts her surface to
moral conventions, no matter what her deeper feelings
may be. The morning-after behavior of Moll and her
Bath lover is precisely what would be expected of newly
fallen innocents—which they are not: "In the Morning

we were both at our Penitentials, I cried very heartily, he express'd himself very sorry" (p. 116). That Moll had long intended to have sexual relations with this man, and that she plans to continue them, is no impediment to her assuming the conventions of penitence. Moll's pretenses of respectability eventually achieve a palpable reality. When importuned to marry the bank clerk, she responds with almost incontrovertible evidence of innocent confusion: ". . . what do you mean, *says I*, colouring a little, what in an Inn, and upon the Road" (p. 180)! She pretends that she wants to be married in a church (where else!). Although Moll is aware of her hypocrisy, the blush is real. She simulates proper responses so devotedly that they acquire a reality of their own.

As her life becomes more openly corrupt, Moll's attempts to hide her evil lead to inner chaos. In her "Terror of Mind" at her first theft, she cries, "Lord . . . what am I now? a Thief" (p. 192)! She calls her "evil Counsellor" the Devil, but she knows that he is "within" (p. 193). To continue to deny her increasingly apparent evil requires enormous effort. Her disguises multiply, and she loses her sense of her own coherence. She takes risks beyond reason, stealing anything, even a horse that she cannot use or sell. Having suppressed those structures provided by the human community, she retains only an inchoate self.

Newgate is the emblem of what Moll has become. Many of Moll's experiences shortly before her imprisonment suggest metaphorically her literal condition at Newgate. One of her last disguises is the beggar's rags that she finds "Ominous and Threatning" (p. 254): "I naturally abhorr'd Dirt and Rags; I had been bred up Tite and Cleanly, and could be no other, whatever Condition I was in" (p. 253). But in prison "I was become a meer *Newgate-Bird,* as Wicked and as Outragious as any of them; nay, I scarce retain'd the Habit and Custom of good Breeding, and Manners, which all along till now run thro' my Conversation; so thoro' a Degeneracy had possess'd me, that I was no more the same thing that I had been, than if I had never been otherwise that what I was now" (p. 279). She is astonished at her irrational adaptation to the place "that had so long expected me" (p. 273): "It is scarce possible to imagine that our Natures should be capable of so much Degeneracy, as to make that pleasant and agreeable that in itself is the most compleat Misery" (p. 278).

Moll feels her impotence in Newgate, where she has "no Friends to assist" (p. 286). One is reminded of a former claustrophobic image, the featherbed that is thrown upon Moll while she is trying to steal goods from a burning house: ". . . nor did the People concern themselves much to deliver me from it, or to recover me at all; but I lay like one Dead and neglected a good while" (p. 224). Moll has in fact lost control of her life well before her capture. She steals what she does not need, even while she is terrorized by the possible consequences of her theft. She almost recognizes her own compulsiveness after the gambling episode: she wins, but will not continue for fear of the "Itch of Play." Immediately she thinks too of ceasing to steal, but, instead, she "grew more hardn'd and audacious than ever" (p. 262).

Moll's repentance is the most detailed one in Defoe's novels.[5] She must not only be brought to reject her evil

[5] See George A. Starr, *Defoe and Spiritual Autobiography* (Princeton: Princeton University Press, 1965), passim, for discussion of the traditional process of repentance.

It seems likely to me that Defoe rewrote and expanded this section. First, Defoe seems to have intended to end the repentance in America. There, Moll's "Heart began to look up more seriously, than I think it ever did before" (p. 336), a statement not compatible with the long section on repentance in Newgate.

past but also be made human again: "I degenerated into
Stone; I turn'd first Stupid and Senseless, then Brutish
and thoughtless, and at last raving Mad" (p. 278). The
focus is on Moll's emotions, not on religious abstractions: "the terror of my mind"; "I look'd on myself as
lost"; "overwhelm'd with melancholy and Despair" ;
"horror to my Imagination"; "how did the harden'd
Wretches . . . Triumph over me"; "flouted me with my
Dejections" (pp. 273-274).

Moll repents immediately, "but that Repentance
yielded me no Satisfaction, no Peace, no not in the least"
(p. 274). Moll's past has created a difficult epistemologi-
cal problem for her. Knowing how she has manipulated
her own feelings she cannot trust them now. What
confirmation of her repentance can there be? She is
confined to her solipsistic prison. Her search for the
"satisfaction" and "comfort" of repentance is successful
only after she is sentenced to death (pp. 287-288): she
finally believes in her repentance when it can no longer
serve an earthly purpose.

Moll's repentance partially restores the integrity of
her feelings: they are no longer always subordinate to
her narrow conception of the utilitarian. Essential to
Moll's repentance is the reappearance of Jemy, her
Lancashire husband, in jail. After her first horror at
Newgate, she had become "insensible." Her pain was
so deep that all feeling had to be suppressed—a condition
that she calls "the compleatest Misery on Earth" (p.
279). But when she sees Jemy, she is "call'd . . . back
a little to that thing call'd Sorrow" (p. 279). As she
thinks of her responsibility for Jemy's destruction, "the
first Reflection I made upon the horrid detestable Life
I had liv'd, began to return upon me, and as these things
return'd my abhorrance of the Place I was in, and of
the way of living in it, return'd also" (p. 281).

Newgate brings Moll to herself—but what is she?

Before Newgate she was at least her pretenses. Now she must generate a new identity. She acknowledges, even emphasizes, past wickedness in order to separate the present from the past. The new structure for her life is that of *repentant* criminal. Those transported with her are no longer her fellows: ". . . a Gang of Thirteen, as harden'd vile Creatures as ever Newgate produc'd in my time; and it would really well take up a History longer than mine to describe the degrees of Impudence, and audacious Villany that those Thirteen were arriv'd to" (p. 295).

But repentance in the face of death does not solve the problem of living. Moll must learn again to deal with her world; having no principles, she again parodies respectability. After she leaves Newgate, she begins to transform her past, even as she acknowledges it. She comments of her money, "a worse gotten Estate was scarce ever put together" (p. 312), but then says immediately, "Our greatest Misfortune as to our Stock, was that it was all in Money" (p. 312). She is now a prudent planter, not a thief. In Virginia, she presents a gold watch to her son, but "*did not indeed tell him* that I had stole it from a Gentlewoman's side" (p. 338). A stolen watch is now a token of her properly tender affections for her child.

Moll's ludicrous responses to this child are a significant part of the novel's pattern:

> It was a wretched thing for a Mother thus to see
> her own Son, a handsome comely young Gentleman
> in flourishing Circumstances, and durst not make
> herself known to him; and durst not take any notice
> of him; let any Mother of Children that reads this,
> consider it, and but think with what anguish of
> Mind I restrain'd myself; what yearnings of Soul
> I had in me to embrace him, and weep over him;

and how I thought all my Entrails turn'd within
me, that my very Bowels mov'd, and I knew not
what to do; as I now know not how to express those
Agonies: When he went from me I stood gazing
and trembling, and looking after him as long as I
could see him; then sitting down on the Grass, just
at a Place I had mark'd, I made as if I lay down
to rest me . . . and lying on my Face wept, and kiss'd
the Ground that he had set his Foot on (p. 322).

This passage appeals to purely conventional assumptions about mothers and children. But convention is
no longer something that Moll uses to hide herself but
to create herself. Her meeting with this son is genuinely
"the pleasantest Day" of her life (p. 337).

Moll achieves the benefits of the maternal relationships that she had forfeited; she is now a good mother
with a dutiful son. Her numerous children had been
a nagging difficulty because they asserted continuities
that she wished to deny. (However, there is no evidence
that Moll ever abused her children. She makes substantial efforts to place each in the care of a relative.) Moll's
suppressed feelings are sordidly parodied in her criminal
career: she repeatedly simulates maternal relationships
in order to steal (pp. 194, 205-206, 257-258), and once,
to avoid capture, she pretends to be sitting with her
daughter (p. 217). Having given up any legitimate maternal function of her own, Moll appropriately enough
addresses the "Governess" as "Mother" (p. 174). But
when Moll finally reconstructs her version of the proper
life, she includes a maternal role for herself.

In Virginia, Moll reintegrates two important fragments of her past into her present—Jemy and her
brother. They represent two possible conclusions to
romantic pretense.[6] Moll's relation with her brother

6 See James Walton, "The Romance of Gentility: Defoe's Heroes

turns into loathing; with Jemy, into good fortune and true love. In both cases, Moll's object is a fortune, her method sentimental cliché.

The emotional climax of Moll's courtship by her brother is the scene that he begins by writing with a diamond upon glass, *"You I Love, and you alone"* (pp. 78-79). The scene then proceeds through a series of banalities. Moll, character and narrator, clearly enjoys this occasion: she is pleased by the semblance of feeling and by the feeble wit, both of which she uses to make a good bargain. She never comments on the irony that this romantic lover turns out to be her brother. She is willing to see herself as wicked but not as a comic fool. Nevertheless, when she returns to Virginia, she wishes to come to terms with this part of her past, for reasons not purely economic. This sordid relationship with her brother is eventually transformed by her joy in her son: the legacy of the beastly brother is a beautiful son.

Moll's relation to Jemy also begins with romantic trappings: both pretend true love and good fortune. But soon they learn that they have duped each other. In this case, however, love does not vanish. It is marked by many kisses, many tears, and possibly a supernatural omen (miles away, Jemy hears Moll call after him). But, unromantically, they separate. Many years later, when Moll sees the swashbuckling highwayman in prison, the romance is revived. He recognizes her immediately, and later gives her "such Testimony of Kindness and Affection as I thought were Equal, if not Superior to that at our parting at *Dunstable*" (p. 304). Out of such gestures Moll can construct a grand illusion. She com-

---

and Heroines," *Literary Monographs* 4 (Madison: University of Wisconsin Press, 1971), pp. 89-135, for an extended discussion of Defoe's versions of the romance pattern in *Moll Flanders, Captain Singleton, Colonel Jack,* and *Roxana.*

fortably evades her past—"I TOLD him I far'd the worse
for being taken in the Prison for one *Moll Flanders*"
(p. 298)—and they go to the New World. There, after
some difficulties, he is re-created in the image that Moll
has chosen:

> I took especial care to buy for him all those things
> that I knew he delighted to have; as two good long
> Wigs, two silver hilted Swords, three or four fine
> Fowling pieces, a fine Saddle with Holsters and
> Pistoles very handsome with a Scarlet Cloak; and
> in a Word, every thing I could think of to oblige
> him; and to make him appear, as he really was,
> a very fine Gentleman (p. 340).

On Moll's second visit, Virgina truly becomes a new
world. It is an odd name for her habitation, but she
is able to construct almost anything out of the pieces
of her past. Her past gives her little resistance. The
Colchester brothers are dead, and her good clerk is too.
The governess knows much, but not everything. Even
when Moll is being transported, she still does not tell
the governess that Jemy is her husband of years ago
(p. 310). Somewhere, perhaps, there are still that husband who deserted her and that repentant Bath lover.
But she has little to fear from them. When Moll returns
to England, she knows that her reputation is finally
safe. Now she and Jemy "resolve to spend the Remainder of our Years in sincere Penitence, for the wicked
Lives we have lived" (p. 343). Moll can now begin an
ideal repentance unencumbered by the embarrassing
demands of a past reality.

One final task remains for Moll—writing *Moll
Flanders*. The book serves many of Moll's needs. Confession purges her of guilt. Also, she can savor her past
as she severs herself from it: her obvious pleasure in
her criminal triumphs is excused by the morals that

she now draws. And she can explain her past in ways that will suppress what still frightens her. Now that she need no longer accommodate herself to her past or to financial exigencies, she can organize her life in any way that she chooses to. She can derive from her past whatever stability she needs.

Moll is eloquent about the need to confess. One of her constant complaints is that she has no confidant (although she always seems to be telling people about herself, she knowingly limits and distorts what she tells). The first time that she pieces together her life for anyone is when in Newgate she confesses to the minister. Only then does she obtain "the Comfort of a Penitent": "This honest friendly way of treating me, unlock'd all the Sluces of my Passions: He broke into my very Soul by it; and I unravell'd all the Wickedness of my Life to him: In a word, I gave him an Abridgement of this whole History; I gave him the Picture of my Conduct for 50 Years in Miniature" (p. 288). But this confession does not relieve Moll's by now chronic anxiety. In the future, her terrors linger even when their causes end: ". . . if any Accident had happened to us, we might at last have been very miserable . . . The very thoughts of it gives me some horror, even since the Danger is past" (p. 330).

In Virginia, she is especially disturbed because she cannot communicate her secrets even to Jemy: ". . . this was a thing I knew not how to open to him, and yet having no Body to disclose any part of it to, the Burthen was too heavy for my mind . . ." (p. 325). She speaks feelingly of the "Necessity" of confessing criminal actions:

This Necessity of Nature, is a thing which Works sometimes with such vehemence, in the Minds of those who are guilty of any atrocious Villany; such as secret Murther in particular, that they have been

> oblig'd to Discover it . . . tho' it may be true that
> the divine Justice ought to have the Glory of all
> those Discoveries and Confessions, yet 'tis as certain
> that Providence which ordinarily Works by the
> Hands of Nature, makes use here of the same
> natural Causes to produce those extraordinary Ef-
> fects" (pp. 325-326).

Without denying the possibility of a final and divine
cause, she recognizes the desire for confession as human.

Moll cannot of course fully accept the implication
that she is writing her story for her own gratification;
that would link her too positively to her criminal past.
When her pondering on confession brings her too close
to this truth, she wrenches the story back to its "purpose":

> As the publishing this Account of my Life, is for
> the sake of the just Moral of every part of it, and
> for Instruction, Caution, Warning and Improve-
> ment to every Reader, so this will not pass I hope
> for an unnecessary Digression concerning some
> People, being oblig'd to disclose the greatest Secrets
> either of their own, or other Peoples Affairs (p. 326).

Moll insists that she is the reader's instructor, not his
parishioner—or patient.

Moll's instructions to us often serve to insulate her
from painful episodes of the past. She tells us how she
escaped because a "poor Boy was deliver'd up to the
Rage of the Street" (p. 212), but immediately gives a
practical turn to the account. She explains the art of
capturing pickpockets, "a Direction not of the kindest
Sort to the Fraternity" (p. 213). In dealing with this
event, she suppresses her feelings of guilt, provides a
justification for her confession, and reiterates her separation from her old companions.

Her confession requires a book because she will not

entrust her life to anyone. Not even the reader knows
her real name. "O! what a felicity is it to Mankind ...
that they cannot see into the Hearts of one another!"
she once says to herself (p. 182). Moll avoids psychological explanations for fear that they may destroy her
precarious mental equilibrium. Nevertheless, pressures
that she cannot explain are apparent in much that she
says. Her first theft is prompted by "a Voice spoken
to me over my Shoulder, take the Bundle; be quick;
do it this Moment" (p. 191). Although Moll asserts that
this voice is the Devil's, Defoe's focus is on Moll. Her
subsequent references to the Devil reveal her loss of
rational control of herself: "my Prompter, like a true
Devil" (p. 194); "the Devil put me upon killing the
Child" (p. 194); "the Devil put things into my Head"
(p. 195); "the diligent Devil ... continually prompted
me" (p. 199); "I blindly obeyed his Summons" (p. 199).

Moll's earlier experience among the debtors in the
Mint was unbearable to her. There she saw the compul-
sions, the irrationality bordering madness, that haunts
her ever after:

> [Men] labouring to forget former things, which now
> it was the proper time to remember ... Sinning
> on, as a Remedy for Sin past. ... they did not only
> act against Conscience, but against Nature; they
> put a Rape upon their Temper ... when he has
> Thought and Por'd on it [his condition] till he is
> almost Mad, having no Principles to Support him,
> nothing within him, or above him, to Comfort him;
> but finding it all Darkness on every Side ... he
> repeats the Crime, and thus he goes every Day one
> Step onward of his way to Destruction (p. 65).

These comments are an acute analysis of the condition
to which Moll is inexorably reduced. She is "fill'd with
horror" in the Mint, but she cannot leave the condition

behind with the place. Newgate itself is another version of the Mint: it too is an emblem of an inner state that Moll is perpetually fleeing.

Moll persistently attempts to give rational explanations for her behavior, glossing over the collapse into irrationality that she senses:

> I have often wondered even at my own hardiness another way, that when all my Companions were surpriz'd, and fell so suddainly into the Hand of Justice, and that I so narrowly escap'd, yet I could not all that while enter into one serious Resolution to leave off this Trade; and especially Considering that I was now very far from being poor, that the Temptation of Necessity, which is generally the Introduction of all such wickedness, was now remov'd; for I had near 500 £   by me in ready money, on which I might have liv'd very well, if I had thought fit to have retir'd; but *I say*, I had not so much as the least inclination to leave off; no not so much as I had before when I had but 200 £   before-hand, and when I had no such frightful Examples before my Eyes as these were; From hence 'tis Evident to me, that when once we are harden'd in Crime, no Fear can affect us, no Example give us any warning (pp. 220-221).

The concluding statement is question-begging, but its moral ring and its reduction of the incomprehensible to cliché are precisely what Moll needs to soothe her terrors. She must reduce the past to the cosier dimensions of her present.

In telling her story, Moll persists in using the economic and religious explanations that have already failed to explain her behavior (now of course she has the economic, and is constructing the religious, stability that she once lacked). Her experience among the debtors in the Mint impels her to find money; but what terrified her about the debtors was their psychological, not their financial condition. Her later marriage to the bank clerk is motivated by her respect for his money and his good character. But what really satisfies her is the stability—the stodginess—of the relationship; it is the antithesis of her experience in the Mint. Despite all her attempted explanations, the language that she uses to describe the end of her "utmost Tranquillity" with the clerk suggests that she was, and still is, uncomprehending: ". . . a sudden Blow from an almost invisible Hand, blasted all my Happiness" (p. 189). She explains her subsequent stealing as necessity, but her "distress" begins while the necessity is still internal: ". . . I saw nothing before me but the utmost Distress, and this represented it self so lively to my Thoughts, that it seem'd as if it was come, before it was really very near; also my very Apprehensions doubl'd the Misery, for I fancied every Sixpence that I paid but for a Loaf of Bread, was the last that I had in the World, and that To-morrow I was to fast, and be starv'd to Death" (p. 190). She needs the "Devil" to explain to herself as well as to us her abrupt movement from outward respectability to crime.

Moll clings desperately to the metaphor that she uses to articulate her private needs—money. It is her metonym for love, sanity, and life itself. After the death of the clerk, her money "wasted daily for Subsistence" (p. 190), and as it is not being replenished, she is "bleeding to Death, without the least hope or prospect of help from God or Man" (p. 190). This equation of her body with money is implicit in the description of her declining beauty: ". . . it was past the flourishing time with me when I might expect to be courted for a Mistress; that agreeable part had declin'd some time, and the Ruins only appear'd of what had been" (p. 189). She is now reduced to taking money and goods alone, without even a semblance of love. For a time, stealing itself provides a new stability: the excitement distracts her from herself. But money has gradually been divested of its meanings, and when she has more than enough for subsistence the irrationality of her actions is again forced upon her consciousness. After her repentance, money and love are again joined: she is reunited with Jemy, and becomes a wealthy planter. She has then returned to her earlier condition—but with a difference. She now has the shrewdness that she then lacked.

Moll's life is too complicated for her to understand. She tries to begin anew—again and again. But when the past impinges too insistently on the present, she loses control. She lives so many lives that she does not know which is hers. At the end of her criminal career, her whirlwind of disguises is both a cause and a symbol of her mental state. Madness lurks on the peripheries of her life. Repeatedly Moll uses the phrase "Reason'd me out of my Reason" (pp. 57, 173). The illness consequent on her desertion by the elder Colchester brother leaves her "Weak," "Alter'd," "Melancholly" (p. 42). Later, in Virginia, her brother threatens to put her into a madhouse (p. 97). At the clerk's death, Moll "sat and cried and tormented my self Night and Day; wringing my Hands, and sometimes raving like a distracted woman; and indeed I have often wonder'd it had not affected my Reason, for I had the Vapours to such a degree, that my Understanding was sometime quite lost in fancies and Imaginations" (p. 190). And many who surround her share her instability. Her brother is distracted and attempts suicide. Her clerk's dissolute wife commits suicide. The clerk himself "grew Melancholy and Disconsolate, and from thence Lethargick, and died" (p. 189). Moll's story is designed to banish these threats and provide an understandable order for her life.

In many respects, Moll is an incompetent. Beneath

the bustle and boasting lie indecisiveness and misunder-
standing. She is repeatedly an easy victim of psychological coercion. The elder brother at Colchester refrains
at first from what "they call the last Favour," but "he
made that self denyal of his a plea for all his Freedoms
with me upon other Occasions" (p. 25). When a variation
of the same technique is used on Moll much later, she
remains uncomprehending. Her Bath lover lies in bed
with her but leaves her "innocent" (p. 115). Although
Moll believes that this is a "noble Principle" (p. 115),
she subsequently entices him into a sexual relationship.
From this time on, Moll bears the responsibility for an
affair that he controls. Moll tries desperately to please
him, but after having enjoyed her fully he repents. Moll
never notices that she is being abused. She met this
lover just after her disastrous marriage to her brother.
She enticed her brother into marriage by pretending to
be uninterested and making him sue; as a consequence,
he does not inquire so closely into her finances as he
might otherwise have done; nor can he blame Moll for
cheating him when he discovers the truth about her
fortune (p. 80). At Bath, Moll is trapped by this same
method that she has used on her brother. And the
episode at Bath is linked to her relationship with her
first lover by those guineas that her Bath lover pours
into her lap (p. 112). She repeatedly plays a debased
Danae to some depraved Jove.

Hardheaded practicality is what Moll admires and
tries to simulate, but the "Governess," not Moll, is the
embodiment of this quality. In a spasm of enthusiasm
for figures and accounts, Moll lists all the prices that
the governess charges for maternity care, even those
that have nothing to do with the story. Moll simulates
the respectable economic virtues without understanding
them. In the subsequent discussion, the governess sees
through Moll's mealymouthed evasions; the more Moll

equivocates about her social status, the more clearly
the governess understands her (p. 162). Moll is relieved
to have someone care for her, and the name that Moll
chooses for this woman describes their relationship. The
governess is always what Moll needs: a midwife when
Moll is with child, a fence when Moll steals, a penitent
when Moll repents. Looked at another way, the governess is whatever can profit from Moll. But Moll is not
cheated. She is allowed the comfort of emotional de-
pendence.

From her childhood, Moll looks to the external world
to provide a structure for her life. In contrast to Singleton, she easily becomes part of families, groups, and
societies. But she always discovers that these structures
provide only a pseudo-order. They give her a role to
play, but the only moral imperative implied by them
is that she have a respectable appearance.

The institution that Moll knows best is the law. Her
experiences with it reflect and reinforce her sense that
everything is a manipulable surface. Her first arrest
occurs because a thief is dressed like a widow and so
is she. A mercer swears falsely that Moll is guilty, but
later the real thief is caught. Although there is a certain
justice in Moll's being taken, she plays the partially
justified part of aggrieved innocence with such aplomb
that she manages to extract 200£ from the mercer for
her false arrest. She hires a respectable lawyer, who
lies for her; had the lawyer been a "petty Fogging hedge
Soliciter, or a Man not known, and not in good Reputation, I should have brought it to but little" (p. 29). Before
the meeting for settlement, the lawyer gives her instructions to appear in "good Cloaths, and with some State,
that the *Mercer* might see I was something more than
I seem'd to be that time they had me" (p. 250).

Newgate is the rotten core of the legal system. Thieves
are set free at night to steal for their jailers (p. 326).

Even the smallest comfort has a price; Moll has enough money for a "little dirty Chamber," so that she does not have to be kept in the common cell for condemned prisoners (p. 290). The "ordinary" only tries to collect evidence: ". . . all his Divinity run upon Confessing my Crime" (p. 277). The good minister who visits her warns her to give up hope of life unless she has "very good Friends" (p. 283). After her sentence has been commuted to transportation, she can buy her pardon: ". . . but it could not be done unless with an Expense too heavy for my Purse" (p. 306).

Justice is done at Moll's trial—but *despite* the legal system, witnesses, and judges. The man whose goods were stolen relents but will not withdraw his charge for fear of losing his bond (p. 277). The witnesses lie; they hate Moll, and will say anything to convict her (p. 284). The judges treat her as an old offender, although she is not one "in the sense of the Law" (p. 293). Moll knows that she is guilty, and an old offender too, but she also knows that such matters have little to do with what happens to her. The law is at best a technicality, at worst a means for legal extortion or private vengeance.

Moll finally makes the best of this difficult world. She repents and becomes respectable; however, there are no regenerative miracles. This book embodies a view of events that is not entirely the narrator's. In fact, Defoe seems deliberately to be avoiding some of the limitations of his earlier novels, especially of *Captain Singleton*. Instead of making Moll the sole repository of the wisdom of the book, Defoe allows us to escape her point of view even as she tells the story.

Nevertheless, Defoe's role in the book is not simply that of ironic historian of Moll's consciousness. The ironies of Moll's decline suggest a set of values by which to judge her: love, community, even respectability. But

Moll loses her moral bearings—and her story does too. The writing that describes Moll's life between her first theft and her imprisonment is unusually untidy, even for Defoe. There are repetitions, incidents introduced too early, events without any clear point. In one sense, the confusions in Moll's narration are imitative of her moral and psychological condition at the described period of her life. But early in the book, Defoe clearly took a position outside the narrator. Where is the ironic distance here? Defoe seems to have reverted to the technique of *Robinson Crusoe* and *Captain Singleton*, reducing himself to the limits of his narrator.

On one occasion, Moll robs a drunken gentleman with whom she has just had a sexual encounter—the only whoring, in the narrow sense of the word, that she ever does. The account is given with a series of evaluations of the characters, all confused and contradictory. Moll's first response is contempt for a man who would lust for her: "There is nothing so absurd, so surfeiting, so ridiculous as a Man heated by Wine in his Head, and a wicked Gust in his Inclination together" (p. 226). Swayed by vanity, she decides that he is "a Man of Sense, and of a fine Behavior; a comely handsome Person, a sober solid Countenance, a charming beautiful Face, and everything that cou'd be agreeable" (p. 227). Next, she imagines the possible consequences of his action:

> ... twas ten to one but he had an honest virtuous Wife, and innocent Children, that were anxious for his Safety ... how would he reproach himself with associating himself with a Whore? pick'd up in the worst of all Holes, the Cloister, among the Dirt and Filth of all the Town? how would he be trembling for fear he had got the Pox, for fear a Dart had struck him through his Liver, and hate himself

every time he look'd back upon the Madness and
Brutality of his Debauch (p. 227)?

She seems almost to have forgotten that she is the
woman with whom the man has coupled.

The governess knows the man, and decides to visit
him. Blackmail is the only possible motive, but she
merely entices the man into a visit with Moll. There
is no plausible explanation for the governess's actions.
Moll at first wants nothing further to do with him, but
changes her mind:

> I had a great many Thoughts in my Head about
> my seeing him again, and was often sorry that I
> had refus'd it; I was perswaded that if I had seen
> him, and let him know that I knew him, I should
> have made some Advantage of him, and perhaps
> have had some Maintenance from him; and tho'
> it was a Life wicked enough, yet it was not so full
> Of Danger as this I was engag'd in (p. 235).

When the man is assured that Moll does not suffer from
venereal disease, he visits her regularly and reproves
himself conscientiously for debauching her: "He would
often make just Reflections also upon the crime itself,
and upon the particular Circumstances of it, with respect to himself; how Wine introduc'd the Inclinations,
how the Devil led him to the Place and found out an
Object to tempt him, and he made the Moral always
himself" (p. 237).

There are many possible views of this incident, none
of them consistent. Moll and the governess indiscriminately draw morals and prey on the man. Moll
censures the relationship, but her comments remain
generalized and abstract; she betrays little personal
involvement. The man's own moralizing is cynical. One
can see the incident as an example of Moll's deterio-

ration—her contradictions verge on the schizophrenic. But there is no sense of a perspective imposed from outside Moll's diseased mind.

Defoe's failure in this incident may be without purpose, but it is not without meaning. Although one can argue that Defoe was careless, the unresolved contradictions in the episode are so egregious that he could hardly have been entirely unaware of them. And this episode is one part of a larger section in which Defoe lost the control that characterizes much of *Moll Flanders*: a carefully defined ironic perspective succumbs to the formlessness of Moll's mind. One must suspect that in some sense Defoe shared Moll's confusion.

Moll lacks any sense of a value that is more than appearance. Her early parodies of respectability collapse in Newgate. She begins again, this time excluding from her life the openly criminal behavior that brought about the previous collapse. She then counterfeits—or conjures, perhaps—the values of love and community which are suggested in the earlier parts of the book. Defoe's reliance on parody reveals his difficulty in imagining any authentic values. When Moll disintegrates, Defoe fails to define any moral world that exists outside her consciousness. Like Moll, he presumably accepts a Christian view of repentance and redemption, but one suspects that his theology is at least in part a device for controlling his fears of those energies that he castigates in *Conjugal Lewdness*. Inner chaos must be suppressed by some order, however arbitrary. Defoe is driven to assert out of fear, not out of belief. In this too, he resembles his creature.

V

A Journal of the Plague Year: Fact and Fiction

A Journal of the Plague Year differs in some obvious ways from the two novels that Defoe wrote in the same year—*Moll Flanders* and *Colonel Jack*. The *Journal* describes an historical event, and it does not create a social world like that of Defoe's other novels; consequently, it is often not included in an inventory of his novels. Except for the narrator, characters in the *Journal* are only intermittently, although vividly, presented. They appear briefly and then disappear.

Even those of Defoe's works ordinarily considered to be novels place less emphasis on the social world than the novels of Richardson and Fielding do. In part, this results from Defoe's method of retrospective first-person narration. Richardson's characters are writing to the moment, and give a powerful, if subjective, sense of their social world. Fielding's omniscient narrator presents a wide range of characters interacting in complicated ways. But most of Defoe's narrators write of a past from which they have detached themselves, a past that is often a danger to them, and that is manipulated to serve present subjective needs. Of course Defoe presents externalities vividly and sometimes meticulously, but he always emphasizes the retrospective ordering consciousness of the narrator. Defoe's narrators make an unmaterial, and often immaterial, use of their obtrusive social and physical world.

In some respects, Defoe links Bunyan to Richardson.

For Defoe's characters, as for Bunyan in *Grace Abounding*, the physical world is an obscure indicator of a more important reality. But Defoe's characters never achieve the kind of spiritual certainty that Bunyan does. They remain enmeshed in their possessions, never quite bringing those jumbled lists of material into a spiritual order. In this they resemble Richardson's Pamela, whose propensity for juxtaposing her trivial acquisitions with spiritual realities is unmercifully burlesqued in Fielding's *Shamela*. In one sense, Fielding is a more moral novelist than Defoe or Richardson—he discriminates more precisely between the spirit and the flesh. But then the conflict of spirt with flesh often seems to be mainly theoretical in Fielding's works: the discrimination is easier because the conflict is less intense.

H. F., like Defoe's other narrators, recounts an intensely personal experience; one is increasingly aware of his presence as he describes the course of the plague. His spiritual crisis is central to the book. Defoe was of course interested in the event being described as well as in its narrator. While writing the *Journal*, he was concerned about a possible recurrence of plague in England, and he wrote *Due Preparations For the Plague* as a guide for body and soul in such a catastrophe. This work was published shortly before *A Journal of the Plague Year*, and includes narrative material in support of its admonitions, some of it used in the *Journal*.[1] But the earlier work does not emphasize any single character: the *Journal*'s focus on its central character puts it in the category of fiction. If not a novel, it is at very least more closely related to Defoe's novels than to any other category of his writings.

A Journal of the Plague Year follows historical

---

[1] See Louis Landa's remarks in the "Introduction" to *A Journal of the Plague Year*, ed. Landa (London: Oxford University Press, 1969), pp. xiv-xv. Subsequent references are to this edition.

sources almost scrupulously: in a recent analysis, F. Bastian concludes that "the invented detail . . . is small and inessential."[2] But in the Puritan religious tradition that informs H. F.'s view of reality, historical events have a spiritual meaning. For H. F., the plague is a metaphysically significant experience, not just a physical phenomenon. Defoe's *Journal*, however, has a differing emphasis from the pious writings that are in its background.[3] When H. F. attempts to find a coherent spiritual purpose governing the physical world, material reality presents itself to him so powerfully that he cannot fully reconcile it with his religious assumptions. The disorienting forces of the plague expose the tensions within him, and we see his conflicts and mounting anxiety. The character overshadows the lesson.

The multitude of details about the plague (the "verisimilitude") are brought into relationship with H. F.'s spiritual and psychological development by several means: H. F. structures his account around his repentance of the decision to remain in London; he frequently comments on his not entirely successful attempts to comprehend the nature of morality in a time of plague; he uses many biblical references to suggest spiritual interpretations of physical reality.

H. F. obliquely invites the reader's attention to what

[2] "Defoe's *Journal of the Plague Year* Reconsidered," *RES*, ser. II, 16 (1965), 172. Manuel Schonhorn, "Defoe's *Journal of the Plague Year*: Topography and Intention," *RES*, ser. II, 19 (1968), 387-402, shows that Defoe, in his search for authenticity, even attempted to describe the topography of London before the fire.

[3] J. Paul Hunter, *The Reluctant Pilgrim* (Baltimore: Johns Hopkins Press, 1966), suggests that the *Journal* should be read "in relation to the providence and diary traditions . . ." (p. 204). The *Journal* also contains elements of the "Guide" tradition studied by Hunter. George A. Starr, *Defoe and Spiritual Autobiography* (Princeton: Princeton University Press, 1965), deals with additional background relevant to this work.

is always implicit in the writing—the personal spiritual concern that informs and shapes it: "Such intervals as I had, I employed in reading Books, and in writing down my Memorandums of what occurred to me every Day.... What I wrote of my private Meditations I reserve for private Use, and desire it may not be made publick on any Account whatever" (pp. 76-77). Among the private matters that do appear in the public account are those concerning his choosing to stay in London during the Plague. He reconsiders the implications of his choice and finally repents of it, seeing it as sinful presumption, not trust in God. His changing attitudes reflect his deepening understanding of the human condition in a time of plague.

Self-consciously and defensively, H. F. asserts that he writes of his decision to remain only to give advice to those who may find themselves in a similar situation (p. 8). Yet his initial account is ambiguous, leading to questions rather than to solutions. He advises the reader: "... if he be one that makes Conscience of his Duty, and would be directed what to do in it, namely, that he should keep his Eye upon the particular Providences which occur at that Time, and look upon them complexly, as they regard one another, and as altogether regard the Question before him ..." (p. 10). But he goes on to accept as "providences" events that his brother, "tho' a very Religious Man himself, laught at ... that I should take it as an Intimation from Heaven, that I should not go out of Town, only because I could not hire a Horse to go, or my Fellow was run away that was to attend me, was ridiculous ..." (p. 11).

H. F. is left "greatly oppress'd ... irresolute, and not knowing what to do" (p. 12). At this point, he resorts to bibliomancy—choosing at random a passage from the Bible for advice about the future (pp. 12-13).[4] The

[4] See Rodney M. Baine, *Daniel Defoe and the Supernatural*

passage he reads is in Psalm 91—traditionally thought to have been written by David in time of plague—and its promises of deliverance convince him to remain in town. Bibliomancy was a subject of controversy in Defoe's time. It was commonly accepted that one might be divinely prompted through the Bible. However, one's arbitrarily selecting a passage from the Bible might also be a usurpation of a divine prerogative; the practice could result in a man's choosing or accepting only that which is in accord with his own will. Whatever Defoe thought of bibliomancy generally, he calls attention here to a dubiety in H. F.'s method. H. F. refers only to several verses from this Psalm—the second through the seventh and also the tenth. This emphasized selectivity invites a rereading of the Psalm to see what has been omitted. The first verse places a qualification on the assurances that follow: "He that dwelleth in the secret place of the Most High shall abide under the shadow of the Almighty" (Ps. 91:1). More important, he has omitted verses 11-12: "For he shall give his angels charge over thee, to keep thee in all thy ways. They shall bear thee up in their hands, lest thou dash thy foot against a stone." These are of course the words that Satan quotes when tempting Christ to cast himself down from a pinnacle of the temple, a temptation to presume on God's mercy. Is H. F. to be commended for his trust in God, or is he wrongfully presuming on God's mercy? The narrator's confidence in his decision cannot be the reader's.

    H. F. recognizes his sin and repents. During the initial stage of repentance, he is terror-stricken: "Terrified by those frightful Objects," he spends much time in the "Confession of my Sins, giving my self up to God every Day, and applying to him with Fasting, Humiliation,

(Athens: University of Georgia Press, 1968), pp. 9-11, for a brief discussion of bibliomancy.

and Meditation" (p. 76). His later response to a water-man, who has been genuinely obliged to remain, reveals his increased understanding:

> And here my Heart smote me, suggesting how much better this Poor Man's Foundation was, on which he staid in the Danger, than mine; that he had no where to fly; that he had a Family to bind him to Attendance, which I had not; and mine was meer Presumption, his a true Dependance, and a Courage resting on God: and yet, that he used all possible Caution for his Safety (p. 108).

These are not only temporary emotional outbursts, for he later sets up a "prescription" that condemns his own conduct: "Upon the foot of all these Observations, I must say, that tho' Providence seem'd to direct my Conduct to be otherwise; yet it is my opinion, and I must leave it as a Prescription, (*viz.*) *that the best Physick against the Plague is to run away from it*" (pp. 197-198). And in case his survival should be regarded as a validation of his choice, he states near the end of the *Journal* that those who remained may owe their "Courage to their Ignorance, and despising the Hand of their Maker, which is a criminal kind of Desperation, and not a true Courage" (p. 238). The *Journal* makes clear that H. F.'s decision to remain was wrong. The advice he finally gives is not to imitate his choice but to recognize his folly.[5]

[5] George A. Starr, *Defoe and Casuistry* (Princeton: Princeton University Press, 1971), has analyzed the *Journal* in the context of casuistry. He emphasizes the importance of the narrator: "Stories of what people did and thought, however striking in their own right, are presented as so many hypothetical answers to whatever question is under consideration at the moment; as materials, in other words, which serve to define or defend H. F.'s own position on a given question, and which the reader is invited to weigh as critically, as sympathetically, and as earnestly as if he were in the same

The opening account of the approaching plague supports the internal emphasis that is predominant in the narrator's account of himself.[6] The plague is dealt with secondarily; in the foreground are the confusions of the people:

> It was about the Beginning of *September*, 1664, that I, among the Rest of my Neighbours, heard in ordinary Discourse, that the Plague was return'd again in *Holland*; for it had been very violent there, and particularly at *Amsterdam* and *Roterdam*, in the year 1663, whither *they say*, it was brought some said from *Italy*, others from the *Levant* among some Goods, which were brought from *Candia*; others from *Cyprus*.

What they hear subsequently is also unverifiable, and their apprehensiveness mounts. The plague bills seem to be something they can trust, but it is soon obvious that the seeming veracity of numbers and dates is as confused and confusing as the rumors. After several fluctuations of hope and fear, "All our Extenuations abated," and the reports of low death rates are known to be "all Knavery and Collusion" (p. 6). This diminishing trust in external authority leaves the people with only their own limited and confused perceptions. H. F. includes himself among the confused populace in the

---

circumstances" (p. 57). I differ from Starr in my emphasis on the narrator's failures and subsequent repentance. Starr regards him as "a model of sustained moderation, at once deliberate and devout" (p. 81).

[6] George A. Starr, "Defoe's Prose Style: 1. The Language of Interpretation," *MP* 71 (1974), 281, remarks of the *Journal* that "the emphasis is more on how things are perceived than on what they are in themselves." His study shows that Defoe's "prose does considerably more subjective interpreting of the external world than critics have recognized" (p. 284).

opening pages, and then tells us of his own morally ambiguous decision to remain in London.

As H. F. presents the multitude of details about the plague year, we can see his confusion and anxiety reflected in his manner of narration. The numbers, the lists, the incidents—all are somehow expected to fix the truth, but the truth is evasive. He always sees alternatives, other possibilities that might be relevant, and seems almost temperamentally incapable of reaching a conclusion. His very style frequently reflects his turmoil: "I cou'd give a great many such Stories as these, diverting enough, which in the long Course of that dismal Year, I met with, *that is* heard of, and which are very certain to be true, or very near the Truth; that is to say, true in General, for no Man could at such a Time, learn all the Particulars" (p. 52). The interrupting qualifications and the many dependent clauses characteristically undermine his assertions. He deals with the murder of watchmen in a similar equivocal fashion:

> It is true, the Watchmen were on their Duty, and acting in the Post where they were plac'd by a lawful Authority; and killing any publick legal Officer in the Execution of his Office, is always in the Language of the Law call'd Murther. But as they were not authoriz'd by the Magistrate's Instructions, or by the Power they acted under, to be injurious or abusive, either to the People who were under their Observation, or to any that concern'd themselves for them; so when they did so, they might be said to act themselves, not their Office; to act as private Persons, not as Persons employ'd; and consequently if they brought Mischief upon themselves by such an undue Behaviour, that Mischief was upon their own Heads; and

indeed they had so much the hearty Curses of the People, whether they deserv'd it or not, that whatever befel them no body pitied them, and every Body was apt to say, they deserv'd it, whatever it was (p. 156).

As the clauses pile up, the repeated qualifications finally obscure murder.

In his evaluations of people and policies, he is usually ambiguous and sometimes contradictory. Perhaps the most obvious example is his commentary on the shutting up of houses: "This is one of the Reasons why I believed then, and do believe still, that the shutting up Houses thus by Force . . . was of little or no Service in the Whole; nay, I am of Opinion, it was rather hurtful . . ." (p. 71). But he later writes: "It is most certain, that if by the Shutting up of Houses the sick had not been confin'd, multitudes . . . wou'd ha' been continually running up and down the Streets, and even as it was, a very great number did so, and offer'd all sorts of Violence to those they met, even just as a mad Dog runs on and bites at every one he meets" (pp. 161-162). He refers to the shutting up of houses obsessively and, although generally against it, is unable to rest on any conclusion.

In making other judgments, he has similar difficulties. He distinguishes between physicians and quacks, but they are equally ineffectual: the "Plague defied all Medicine." The physicians go about "prescribing to others and telling them what to do, till the Tokens were upon them, and they dropt down dead, destroyed by that very Enemy, they directed others to oppose" (pp. 35-36). With apparently unintentional irony, he then comments: "Abundance of Quacks too died, who had the Folly to trust their own Medicines . . ." (p. 36). He is unwilling or unable to reach a clear judgment about the clergymen. He is contemptuous of the rabble-rousing predictions of doom by the soothsayers, but must condemn the ministers for similar behavior (pp. 24-25). Those ministers who flee from their charges seem to be blameworthy, but at the end he finds too many complications to be able either to blame or to exculpate them (p. 235). This evasiveness is so persistent that even if one concedes individual cases in which Defoe was merely careless, the overall design cannot be easily explained as fortuitous.

The narrator believes unequivocally that the first cause of the plague is God, although the plague operates in general through natural means (p. 193, for example).[7] But this belief raises other questions. To what end is the city plagued? What should be the effect of the plague on the individual moral life? Although the narrator feels that the plague should bring men to repentance, he notices that while fear causes some to repent it leads many others to "extremes of Folly" (p. 29). And afterward, "it must be acknowledg'd that the general Practice of the People was just as it was before, and very little Difference was to be seen" (p. 229).

What has the most vivid effect upon H. F. is not the repentance of the people but the total moral collapse brought by the plague: "But, alas! this was a Time when every one's private Safety lay so near them, that they had no Room to pity the Distresses of others; for every one had Death, as it were, at his Door. . . . This, I saw,

[7] In considering the causes of the plague, H. F. adopts the usual Puritan view of God's interventions in his providentially ordered universe: God uses natural means to accomplish something beyond the ordinary course of nature. This is a "special Providence," and differs from a "miracle" because it does not set aside the laws of nature. Many Puritans thought that miracles ceased after biblical times. For a full discussion, see Perry Miller, *The New England Mind: The Seventeenth Century* (Cambridge, Mass.: Harvard University Press, 1939), especially pp. 226-229.

took away all Compassion; self Preservation indeed appear'd here to be the first Law" (p. 115). Even parents and children abandon each other (p. 115), and death is a "Deliverance" (p. 98). His grim account of how the deaths of the poor are fortunate for others suggests a new perspective on conventional human feelings and values: ". . . they would in Time have been even driven to the Necessity of plundering either the City it self, or the Country adjacent, to have subsisted themselves, which would first or last, have put the whole Nation, as well as the City, into the utmost Terror and Confusion" (p. 98).

The symbolic and psychological meanings in the account of the "great pit," a mass grave in the churchyard in Aldgate, are relevant to the narrator's attempts to find a moral meaning in the human condition (pp. 58-63). This "terrible Pit" suggests some of the many biblical uses of the image, both literal and figurative. Korah's rebellion against Moses was ended when he and his followers "went down alive into the pit, and the earth closed upon them: and they perished from among the congregation" (Num. 16:33). The Psalmist prays, "Hear me speedily, O Lord: my spirit faileth: hide not thy face from me, lest I be like unto them that go down into the pit" (Ps. 143:7). The symbolic suggestions of the pit, a fearsome death and alienation from God, are underlined by the narrator's calling it a "dreadful Gulph . . . for such it was rather than a Pit" (p. 59), suggesting the "great gulf fixed" between the rich man in hell and Lazarus, who is with Abraham (Luke 16:26).

Because of the danger of infection, it is forbidden to go near the pit. But the narrator "resolv'd to go in the Night and see some of them thrown in" (p. 60), an example of the seemingly brutal curiosity that sometimes inspires him. With the argument that "it might be an Instructing Sight," he gains admittance, the sexton responding, "'Tis a speaking Sight ... and has a Voice with it, and a loud one, to call us all to Repentance ..." (p. 61). The narrator's curiosity about the appalling sight is not idle: he desires, in the fullest metaphoric sense, to see into the pit, to comprehend the plague and the human condition that it reveals. This desire becomes a compulsion. After the plague intensifies, H. F. admits that he need not leave his house; nevertheless, "tho' I confin'd my Family, I could not prevail upon my unsatisfy'd Curiosity to stay within entirely my self; and tho' I generally came frighted and terrified Home, yet I cou'd not restrain; only that indeed, I did not do it so frequently as at first" (p. 80).

The same night in which he visits the pit, H. F. has an altercation with the "dreadful Set of Fellows" at the Pye-Tavern (p. 64). The tavern is "within View of the Church Door" (p. 67), but the men mock those who attend public worship and laugh at the narrator's "calling the Plague the Hand of God" (p. 66). H. F. is presented with two possible responses to the plague—that of the tavern or that of the Church. This episode is related to the story of Korah. Several accounts of people going alive into the pit had previously been mentioned, and the roisterers taunt the "poor Gentleman," about whom the narrator is concerned, "with want of Courage to leap into the great Pit, and go to Heaven ..." (p. 64). The narrator leaves their company "lest the Hand of that Judgment which had visited the whole City should glorify his Vengeance upon them, and all that were near them" (p. 66). He follows the advice of Moses to those near Korah and his followers: "Depart, I pray you, from the tents of these wicked men, and touch nothing of theirs, lest ye be consumed in all their sins" (Num. 16:26). The men of the tavern do meet the end of Korah, thus vindicating the narrator's faith in a controlling moral order: "... they were every one of them carried into the great Pit, which I have mentioned above, before it was quite fill'd up, which was not above a Fortnight or thereabout" (pp. 66-67).

But this episode is not a resolution of the questions that have preoccupied H. F. Although his faith in a moral scheme is confirmed, he continues to be baffled in his attempts to understand the complexities of divine justice. Also at this time, his concern turns more profoundly inward: he seriously wonders whether he rebuked the men at the Pye-Tavern for pious or for egotistical reasons (p. 69). Although he finally vindicates himself, his self-assurance is shaken. Shortly thereafter, he endures the first terror-filled stage of his repentance (p. 76).

Biblical allusions and parallels give even the seemingly circumstantial accounts a spiritual dimension. Many traditional typological interpretations were accepted by the dissenters; and in the seventeenth century, typology was frequently extended to postbiblical history. Biblical types could be prefigurations not only of later biblical events but also of later history. In J. Paul Hunter's words, ". . . the broadened typology offered contemporary history an extended mythic dimension based upon past history frozen into static form."[8] The plague and the great fire almost demanded typological treatment. "Plague" itself is the term persistently used in the English Bible for God's judgments, especially those on the Egyptians before the Exodus and on the Israelites afterward. Fire is another common image of God's judgments, especially of those that are final, and the narrator refers frequently to the fire that will destroy London after the plague. His prophetic tone suggests the apocalyptic: "But the Time was not fully

[8] *The Reluctant Pilgrim*, pp. 100-101. See the entire discussion, pp. 99-102.

come, that the City was to be purg'd by Fire, nor was
it far off; for within Nine Months more I saw it all
lying in Ashes . . ." (p. 243; see 2 Pet. 3:11-12).

The narrator specifically suggests a relationship between the conduct of the Israelites and that of the
Londoners: ". . . it might too justly be said of them,
as was said of the Children of *Israel*, after their being
delivered from the Host of *Pharaoh*, when they passed
the *Red-Sea*, and look'd back, and saw the *Egyptians*
overwhelmed in the Water, *viz.* That *they sang his
Praise, but they soon forgot his Works*" (p. 248). The
wanderings of Israel were usually interpreted typologically as the spiritual journey of Everyman. For example,
Matthew Henry, author of a Bible commentary that
was respected in Defoe's time, remarks of the Red Sea:
"Israel's passage through it was typical of the conversion
of souls, (Isa. xi.15) and the Egyptian's perdition in it
was typical of the final ruin of all impenitent sinners,
Rev. xx.14."[9] Defoe's allusion is directed to the historical
situation of London after the plague and also to the
spiritual condition of individuals.

Some of the allusions relate London to the cities of
Nineveh and, more important, Jerusalem. Nineveh suggests the possibility of repentance (p. 29). Jerusalem is
related, however, to repeated and increasing punish-
ments: the dispersions of the Jews; the occupation of
the city and the profanation of the temple by Antiochus
Epiphanes; and the conquest by Titus. The narrator
refers specifically to Jeremiah's comments on Jerusalem's impending doom (pp. 68, 193) and to the later
destruction by the Romans (pp. 18, 21). In addition,
he alludes to biblical passages traditionally interpreted
as prophetic of the destruction of Jerusalem. The reference to Josephus's account of a man crying "woe to

[9] *An Exposition of the Old and New Testament* (1st American
ed.; Philadelphia: Barrington and Haswell, 1828), 1:281.

Jerusalem" (p. 21) suggests Christ's mourning for Jerusalem (Matt. 23:37-39; Mark 13:1-2). Christ's prophetic
warnings are also mentioned as applicable to Londoners
in plague: *"Wo! be to those who are with Child: and
to those which give suck in that Day"* (p. 118; Matt.
24:19). A related allusion occurs in H. F.'s meeting with
the waterman, who has been obliged to remain in London with his wife and family. His wife's name is Rachel,
and their child has plague (pp. 108-109), details that
are reminiscent of Jeremiah's prophecy: "A voice was
heard in Ramah, lamentation, and bitter weeping; Rachel weeping for her children refused to be comforted
for her children, because they were not" (Jer. 31:15;
cf. Matt. 2:16-18).

These references are connected with the narrator's
specific situation as well as generally with the city. In
each of the gospels in which Christ prophesies the
destruction of Jerusalem, he also warns his listeners to
flee (Matt. 2:16; Mark 13:14; Luke 21:21); woes are
predicted for those who cannot flee—for example, those
who are with child. The story of the three men from
Stepney parish—the soldier, the sailor, and the carpen-
ter—reinforces the warning implied by these allusions.
As F. Bastian notes, "No effort is made to fit the story
convincingly into the rest, by pretending, for instance,
that H. F. was connected with any of the participants."[10]
However, the story is thematically relevant; the decision
of these men to leave is the appropriate one, and provides
an indirect comment on H. F.

In his introduction to the story of the three men,
H. F. implies that he thinks of the account as having
a moral significance that goes beyond its literal one.
His first, abortive, introduction states that even if the
plague does not return, "still the Story may have its
Uses so many Ways as that it will, I hope, never be

[10] "Defoe's *Journal of the Plague Year* Reconsidered," p. 170.

said, that the relating has been unprofitable" (p. 58). Later, just before he actually begins the story, he not only recommends the conduct of these men as a pattern to follow in time of plague but also states that the "Story has a Moral in every Part of it . . ." (p. 127). The broad outlines are obviously parallel to the biblical account of the Israelites leaving Egypt to find the Promised Land, typologically mankind seeking salvation. The men flee a plague-stricken city, and live nomadically in a hostile environment. Eventually they and their company establish themselves in an abandoned house, where they remain until the plague has abated. What the story seems to inculcate is the personal effort that, in addition to reliance on God, is necessary for salvation. H. F.'s passive trust in God is presumptuous.

There are other more explicit biblical references in this story. After the wanderers are given wheat, they must eat it "in parched Corn, as the *Israelites* of old did without grinding or making Bread of it" (p. 146), an allusion to the Israelites before the city of Jericho (Josh. 5:11). The major difficulties that the wanderers from Stepney parish face are those of finding food and gaining permission to pass through towns (p. 123). Finding food is a recurrent difficulty for the Israelites, and both the Edomites and Amorites refuse to allow passage, even though the Israelites offer to "go by the high way: and if I and my cattle drink of thy water, then I will pay for it: I will only, without doing anything else, go through on my feet" (Num. 20:19; see also 21:22-23; see also *Journal*, pp. 134-135).

The care with which Defoe's allusions are selected is attested to by the pertinence of even the seemingly casual reference to the lepers of Samaria. The old soldier John says, *"I am of the same Mind with the Lepers of Samaria: 'If we stay here we are sure to die'"* (p. 124). The complete story of these lepers is found in 2

Kings 7. The Israelites, besieged by the Syrians, had no food. In desperation, the lepers among them went to the Syrian camp, where they discovered that the Syrians had fled, leaving plenty of food: "For the Lord had made the host of the Syrians to hear a noise of chariots, and a noise of horses, even the noise of a great host . . ." (2 Kings 7:6). This same John who mentions the lepers subsequently devises the strategem by which the wanderers, pretending to be a large armed band, get food from the people of Walthamstow (pp. 135-139). This is another example of the recommended combination of personal effort and divine prompting.

H. F.'s advice—*"the best Physick against the plague is to run away from it"* (pp. 197-198)—reflects not only his increased understanding but also the limits of his understanding. He sees the plague as a terrifying evil that frustrates his attempts at moral discriminations. The prophecies of Christ that H. F. alludes to cannot increase his understanding greatly. Christ's injunction is to flee; although there is an overall moral order, no promises are made to those unable to flee: woes are pronounced upon them, no matter how morally worthy they may be. This sense of a judgment that evades man's usual moral discriminations pervades *A Journal of the Plague Year*, and produces the anxiety in the narrator that is so common among Defoe's characters. One of the frequently repeated words in Defoe's writings is "hardened," and the ultimate evil is the hardened heart that cannot respond to God's judgments.[11] The narrator of the *Journal* seeks calm, but he cannot confidently distinguish this state from hardening. He alternates between trust and fear, seeking to escape his terrors

[11] See Starr's chapter on *Moll Flanders* in *Defoe and Spiritual Autobiography* for a discussion of "the classic process of hardening" (p. 137).

but also believing them to be evidence of his respon-
siveness to God.

It is the intensity of the focus on the narrator that
makes *A Journal of the Plague Year* something more
like a novel than like either history or the seven-
teenth-century pious writings that lie in the background. *The Pilgrim's Progress* continues to be interesting because of its Christian, but he is contained within
the boundaries of the work's didacticism. H. F.'s attempts to instruct the reader frequently become evidence of his psychological turmoil; although the lesson
is poorly taught, the character's emotional difficulties
are powerfully communicated. *A Journal of the Plague
Year* contains signs of the hasty writing that flaws so
much of Defoe, but the aptness of the allusions and
the clear development of H. F. suggest a coherent design.
Indeed, the allusions are more precisely used here than
in any other of Defoe's fictional works. Defoe organizes
his factual material to suggest a spiritual reality that
lies beyond the physical one. But instead of directing
the spiritual meanings primarily outward toward the
reader for a didactic purpose, Defoe uses these meanings
to create a psychologically complex and interesting
central character.

Defoe's relationship to his narrator seems less ambiguous than usual in this work. H. F. is never quite explicit
about all his earlier failures. We are to see ironies that
he is not entirely aware of. But he develops into a more
perceptive man, one whose view of things is to be taken
seriously. In his didactic works, Defoe usually takes a
more stentorian moral tone than H. F.'s, but here H.
F.'s vacillations are treated sympathetically. Like
Defoe's other narrators, he is unable to grasp final moral
truths in his appalling situation, but his eventual spiritual and emotional condition seems less unstable than

theirs. A continuing moral struggle is, after all, acceptable, even desirable, in the Puritan tradition.

Moll and Colonel Jack, the two other characters that Defoe created in the year of the *Journal*, impose unconvincing spiritual patterns on their lives as they narrate them. The imposed patterns serve their needs to settle the past in a way that will not interfere with present satisfactions. Moll and Jack are shown to be misusing religious assumptions that Defoe presumably accepts. Nevertheless, their failure to find a clear spiritual pattern in their lives implies that these assumptions themselves are questionable. In reading the *Journal*, one is less conscious of a Defoe who is undermining his own beliefs.

The *Journal*, however, is not incongruous with the other novels: H. F. answers the ultimate questions no more convincingly than Defoe's other characters do. But the plague is brief and violent; we do not expect H. F. to solve the problem of evil in a providentially ordered world while he is enduring his terrible experience. The plague is one of those anomalous events that made even a man like Job question God's order. In his other novels, which are not rooted in cataclysmic historical events, Defoe has to imagine a world less clearly related to the metaphors of traditional spiritual experience. The plague provides Defoe with an interpretation as well as an event. The imagination reflected in the *Journal* is both more limited and more coherent than that reflected in his other novels.

VI

Colonel Jack:

Heroic and Mock-Heroic

Defoe's works are often explorations of failing metaphors. His characters choose some term to articulate their demands of life, and for a time this term provides a sense of identity and destiny. But the metaphoric equation almost inevitably collapses, and the character glimpses the obsessive nature of his actions. He is compelled, like the narrator of *A Journal of the Plague Year*, to look into the abyss, where all that he sees with certainty is himself. His terror then leads him to reconstruct his metaphor. A solipsistic meaning, a purely verbal construct, is more bearable than a contemptible self in a meaningless world.

These various metaphors become the motifs of Defoe's works: they are repeated, and each character has his dominant one. Crusoe's is travel; Singleton's, trade; Moll's, gold; and Colonel Jack's, gentility. H. F. is a special case; his metaphor is the plague, and it leads him directly to the metaphysical questions that are avoided by the other characters. But H. F.'s metaphor concludes literally, and he too can then lapse into quiescence. In the other cases, each character's emotional stability is dependent upon his preventing his metaphor from collapsing: insanity, always lurking on the fringes of Defoe's created world, must be exorcised by words.

Word play is present throughout Defoe's works, but

it is especially prominent in *Moll Flanders*, which is an exploration of Moll's linkings of money and love. There is much significant verbal repetition. "Undone," for example, first suggests sexual and spiritual disaster, but is finally shorn of any moral meaning, referring only to financial failure (*M. F.*, p. 65). The verbal texture of *Moll Flanders* is a matter not only of sustained metaphor but also of merely local punning, often gratuitous and jocular, as in Moll's reference to "my Friends the Quakers" (*M. F.*, p. 264). This kind of word play calls attention to the verbal surface, and emphasizes the concern with simulation and parody—with verbal maneuvering—that is implicit in the book.[1]

The metaphors of Defoe's novels are often implicit as well as explicit: the narrator is not conscious that his conceptions are merely figurative. Indeed, words become not the narrator's figures but his reality. Incident after incident in *Colonel Jack* shows the central character's behavior being guided by his notions of gentility. His whole life becomes an attempt to concretize what we know is only his metaphor for deeper aspirations. Love, war, money, clothes, titles—none are significant to Colonel Jack except as attempts to find a reality corresponding to some dimly apprehended but disembodied conception.

Not only Colonel Jack but also Moll Flanders and Roxana inhabit a world that often seems almost entirely contructed of such self-deluding metaphors. Defoe, we assume, believed in an ultimate spiritual reality that informed the appearances of his world; repentance to him was presumably more than a verbal trick. But with increasing clarity, he displays his characters' self-deceptions. Even repentance seems to be only the character's

[1] Maximillian Novak, "Defoe's 'Indifferent Monitor': The Complexity of *Moll Flanders*," ECS 3 (1970), 351-365, gives many examples of word play in *Moll Flanders*.

last effort to find another set of words to obscure the truth about himself.

The word "gentleman" is reiterated throughout *Colonel Jack* in a wide range of contexts. The central figure never vacillates in his commitment to this word despite his varying conceptions of its meaning. To him it is the summation of all felicity. "Gentlemen, Do ye call?" cry the waiters as the ragamuffins, Jack and his friend, eat their dinner of boiled beef. To Jack "this was as good . . . as all my Dinner" (p. 16).[2] He questions money as the end of life, but not gentility (p. 67).

Jack's career as a thief is described by analogies to social rank. He is first apprenticed to a "Pick-pocket above the ordinary Rank" (p. 18), and eventually he is introduced to a gang of housebreakers "where . . . we shall be all Gentlemen" (p. 59). Defoe fully exploits the conventional ironic verbal equation of gentleman and criminal. Although Jack evades the gallows, his rise is still a fall.

In childhood, Jack senses the possibilities entailed in his nothingness: ". . . I was left to call myself Mr. Anything, what I pleas'd, as Fortune and better Circumstances should give occasion" (p. 4). He chooses like a dutiful son to do as his unknown father bade— *"remember, that I was a Gentleman"* (p. 3). Doing so is difficult; not only does he not know what a gentleman is, but he develops none of the traditional allegiances to Church and country to guide him. He knows that he differs from his criminal friends; yet his conception is unembodied, almost mystical. It is only a word attached to indefinable longings: ". . . my Gentleman . . . was another thing quite, tho' I cou'd not really tell how to describe it neither" (p. 62).

But assiduously Jack forms himself according to those

[2] *Colonel Jack*, ed. Samuel Holt Monk (London: Oxford University Press, 1965). Subsequent references are to this edition.

notions that he acquires. Once he hears a man reproved
for swearing ("is this like a Gentleman"), and ceases
swearing, not out of moral principle but in imitation
of this meaning for "gentleman" (p. 61). Often his
pursuit of gentility is laughably enmeshed in his ungentlemanly life. He begins to wear a hat after being
treated contemptuously for wearing rags (p. 27), but
the hat becomes a receptacle for stolen money (p. 44).
He wants to learn to read—in order to tell if he is the
one named on a warrant (p. 80). He resumes his education when he is over thirty (p. 157), and then reads the
martial stories that he emulates so unsuccessfully in
his European adventures. Jack's conception of a gentleman is not incongruous with that of the warehouse
keeper in Virginia who gives him a suit of clothes and
says, "go in there a Slave, and come out a Gentleman"
(p. 127).

"Colonel" is his most insistent claim to gentility. He
gets the name as a result of childish squabbling, and
it provides him with at least another name to go with
Jack. His unknown father was also reputed to be a
colonel. In these rather vague hints, Colonel Jack senses
a destiny, although one not entirely compatible with
his genius: "I pass'd among my Comrades for a bold
resolute Boy, and one that durst fight any thing; but
I had a different Opinion of my self, and therefore
shunn'd Fighting as much as I could" (p. 7).

His military career is almost as inauspicious as its
beginning promises. He deserts a Scotch regiment after
it is ordered to Flanders, where he will "be knock'd on
the Head at the Tune of Three and Six-pence a Week"
(p. 105). Many years later he observes King William's
forces and the French, after he is given the opportunity
to see the "Service ... without much Hazard" (p. 183).
He has little enthusiasm for either side, and returns
to England, where he masquerades as the French Colo-

nel Jacques, a typical instance of his patriotism (pp. 185-186).

He later becomes a captain, and achieves a reputation for bravery: "... they Flattered me so with my bravery as they call'd it on the Occasion of this Action, that I fancy'd myself Brave, whether I was so or not, and the Pride of it made me Bold, and Daring to the last Degree on all Occasions" (p. 208). He subsequently describes more looting than valor, including one comic conundrum created by his insistence on the forms of chivalry, even when they have no attachment to any substance. He has been captured by an officer who is "so generous to me, as not to ask what Money I had about me" (p. 215). Jack recaptures this officer, but he has "lost by his Civility, for then I could not have the Assurance to ask him for his Money" (p. 215).

He has enough of war when he is shot and also knocked down, the foot soldier's fate that he had hoped to avoid by becoming an officer (p. 129). However, he cannot just quit, because "it was counted so Dishonourable a Thing to quit, while the Army was in the Field" (p. 222). His solution is to volunteer in the Jacobite cause. He pretends "a great deal of Zeal" (p. 222), although he has "no particular attachment" to the Chevalier (p. 223). Nevertheless, he is treated with respect, and obviously begins to think of himself as a dashing cavalier. And he even expects to become a colonel when he arrives in England (p. 222). But the invasion is a disaster, and he returns to Dunkirk, thinking of nothing but "Halters and Gibbets" (p. 224). This experience brings Colonel Jack as close to "colonel" as he ever comes.

Jacobitism appeals to his social pretensions. Despite his earlier coolness to the cause, he becomes a hot Jacobite before the Battle of Preston—although he does of course manage to miss the battle. When he later sees

some of the transported men from Preston, he calls their
condition "Slavery—which to Gentlemen must be worse
than Death" (p. 251). The comment is a strange one
to come from someone who recommends indenture in
Virginia as a good way to begin life again. In his
maturity, the thought of "gentleman" never fails to
evoke a cliché from Colonel Jack. He will not have any
of the Preston men as servants, "pretending that I would
not make Slaves every Day of unfortunate gentlemen,
who fell into that Condition, for their Zeal to their Party
only" (p. 266). He is not blind to his hypocrisy; his "true
Reason" is that he "expected several of them would
know me, and might perhaps betray me" (p. 266). Here,
as elsewhere, he economically combines social preten-
sion and self-preservation.

He is even less successful in love than in war. He
attempts to find ladies to whom he can display his
cavalier charms, but the ladies turn out to be as unsuit-
able as his charm is bogus. Jack's first relationship with
a woman occurs when he is over thirty and "knew the
least of what belong'd to a Woman, of any Man in
Europe of my Age" (p. 186), a comment presumably
intended to explain his subsequent behavior. He describes the relationship in military metaphors, but he
is no courtly lover just as he is no soldier (pp. 187, 193).
The lady is only a trollop, but Jack is totally deceived—
he seems to think that he is playing Antony to a
Cleopatra: ". . . she had such a Stock of bitterness upon
her Tongue, as no Woman ever went beyond her, and
yet all this while she was the pleasantest, and most
obliging creature in every Part of our Conversation"
(p. 189). Defoe calls attention to her vulgarity after Jack
marries her: "Drop'd her Burthen, *as she call'd it*" (p.
195, and see pp. 194-195 passim). During courtship, Jack
is proud of being none of the "whining Sort of Lovers"
(p. 189); instead, he is sullen. His attempts at courtship

occasionally resemble gallantry, but they are only the mawkish truth: "... I hated you because you would never give me an Opportunity to tell you I lov'd you" (p. 192).

After he is openly and contemptuously cuckolded and deserted (p. 196), it occurs to this cavalier to sell his "Furniture by Publick out-cry, and in it every thing in particular that was her own, and set a Bill upon my Door, giving her to understand by it, that she had pass'd *the Rubicon*" (p. 197). Passed the Rubicon! When Jack subsequently persists in his tradesmanly revenge of not giving her any money, he is visited by a "Gentleman well Dress'd," who informs him that merchants pay and gentlemen fight (pp. 199-200). Not wanting to do either ("tho' I had learn'd a great many good things in *France* to make me look like a Gentleman; I had forgot the main Article, of learning, how to use a Sword"), Jack suggests a resolution by law (pp. 200-201). Ludicrously suggesting that he is maintaining Jack's wife's nonexistent honor (p. 201), the gentleman shortly thereafter has Jack's nose slit and his ear cut (p. 204). This confrontation of gentleman and merchant exposes both Jack's ineptitude and the grossness of the "gentlemanly" code; nevertheless, Jack is not deterred in his search for gentility. He learns to use a sword.

The next time that he is cuckolded (that is, the next time he marries), he seriously wounds the offender in a duel. But he remains a comic butt. He marries this woman because of a drunken promise made after he has debauched her (pp. 221-222). Even after he is certain that she is unfaithful, he pretends it is not happening:

[his wife and her lover] talk'd of casual things, of a young Lady a Burgher's Daughter of 19, that had been Married the week before to an Advocate in the Parliament of *Paris*, vastly Rich, and about

63, and of another, a Widow Lady of Fortune in
Paris, that had married her deceas'd Husbands
Valet de Chamber, and of such casual Matters, that
I could find no Fault with now at all (p. 226).

He wants a wife who will satisfy his social ambitions;
yet in every case the desire is thwarted. When he finally
does find a wife who is "every way most exquisitely
Genteel" (p. 238), her behavior subsequently becomes
grossly scandalous. As a result of illness, she drinks
liquors immoderately:

> ... till instead of a well made, fine Shape, she was
> as Fat as an Hostess. ... In short, she lost her
> Beauty, her Shape, her Manners, and at last her
> Virtue ... in which Time she twice was exposed
> in the most scandalous manner, with a Captain of
> a Ship, who like a Villain, took the Advantage of
> her being in Drink, and not knowing what she did:
> but it had this unhappy Effect, that instead of her
> being asham'd, and repenting of it, when she came
> to her self; it harden'd her in the Crime, and she
> grew as void of Modesty at last as of Sobriety (pp.
> 240-241).

This relationship had begun with rituals of gentility
sufficient to satisfy even Jack's inordinate desires. Sup-
pers, proposals, and marriage were managed precisely
and with all possible delicacy.

In revulsion, Jack next marries Moggy, who seems
to have no pretensions at all. But she does have at least
one pretense—after her death, Jack learns of her bastard
(p. 249). He then remarks with some philosophy, "such
was my Fate in Wives." He had, after all, been happier
with Moggy than with any other wife. However, Jack's
aspirations are undiminished. Experience never affects
his commitment to his goal—the life of a gentleman.

The equanimity that he displays after discovering Moggy's past is rare. His life is a succession of fears punctuated by outbursts of rage. By his violence, he revenges the quivering physical fear of which he is so conscious. Although "frighted to the last degree," he attacks the gentleman who wishes to duel: ". . . had not the Constable step'd in, and taken me off, I had certainly stamp'd him to Death, with my Feet" (pp. 202-203). At his second cuckolding, he rages in imagination (he is still not anxious to duel): ". . . I had no Government of myself . . . I committed Murther more than once, or indeed than a hundred times, in my imagination" (p. 225). He wishes to lose no credit for his violent imagination and occasional violent deeds; he narrates them in detail, and they provide a counterpoise to his cowardice.

The device of the three Jacks who grow up together—the captain, the major, and the colonel—is used to present the alternatives for Colonel Jack. Although he becomes a criminal, the major has some of the gentlemanly virtues, "a true Manly Courage" with gentleness and compassion (p. 6). The captain is unmitigated force, "brutish, bloody, and cruel in his Disposition . . . the Nature of a Bull Dog, bold and desperate, but not generous at all" (p. 5). Colonel Jack's essential quality is shrewd evasiveness: ". . . I many times brought my self off with my Tongue, where my Hands would not have been sufficient; and this as well after I was a Man, as while I was a Boy" (p. 7). He clearly longs for the major's attractive qualities, but he also admires the captain's unqualified rage. He attempts to organize, or at least to simulate, all these traits in one personality.

The major disappears early from an active part in the story. But the captain is so persistently present that one can scarcely avoid seeing him as a projection of a Colonel Jack unrestrained by fear. The two continue together, seemingly despite their wishes (pp. 98, 103).

The colonel objects to the captain's open criminality, but both live on the captain's thefts, the colonel even sharing a stolen horse (p. 89). The essential distinction between them is that the colonel is a "wary Politick Gentleman" who devises schemes that are almost safe although not quite honest (p. 91).

When they are kidnapped, the captain responds with implacable rage, totally unrestrained by the ship's master's authority: ". . . I have promis'd you to cut your Throat, and depend upon it I will be as good as my Word" (p. 116). Colonel Jack admires the captain's intrepidity (p. 113), but being "Politick," he realizes that the captain's future is grim. Both captain and major defy society and are destroyed: the captain is hanged in England, and the gallant major has the "Honour to be broke upon the Wheel at the *Greve* in *Paris*" (pp. 184-185). The colonel sees that submission—real or pretended—is necessary. He must at least acknowledge the premises of the society that he wishes above all to enter.

Through submission, Jack rises to become overseer in Virginia. The whip that was his own "Terror but the Day before" (p. 128) is now his to wield. But his first attempt reveals his usual ineffectuality: ". . . after I had Lash'd them till every Blow I struck them, hurt my self, and I was ready to Faint at the Work, the Rogues Laught at me, and one of them had the Impudence to say behind my Back, that if he had the Whipping of me, he would show me better how to Whip a *Negro*" (p. 128).

Jack then devises a more effective method for dealing with the slaves—terror. He first puts them "under the terrible Apprehensions of a Punishment, so Severe, as no *Negro* ever had before" (p. 134). Then they are pardoned by an absent "Great Master." Colonel Jack pretends to have solicited the pardon, and the slaves are forever grateful to both master and overseer. The

object of this charade is "to imprint Principles of Gratitude on their Minds" (p. 134)—and make them work
hard.

This trick is explained in the language of morality
and emotion: slaves are capable of "gratitude" and Jack
is "merciful." But there is no mercy, only the "method"
of mercy (p. 146), just as there is no gratitude, only
relief from fear. When Jack pretends to wish to serve
his master out of "Gratitude," the man replies that he
"will not be serv'd upon those terms" (p. 148). Both
he and Jack understand the debased conception of
self-interest underlying their moral palaver. Jack flatters his master in order to get help, and the master
finds it profitable to help a valuable servant (p. 148).

However, neither Jack nor the master is merely practical. Their seemingly humanitarian principles are used
to disguise fear and hatred. The discussion between
them, in which Jack's methods are explained, is in
dialogue with the speakers labeled as in a script. The
effect is histrionic: private motives seep through the
public demonstration.

Jack cannot effectively punish the slaves because he
fears both them and his own whip (Jack has feared the
whip ever since in childhood he saw the brutal captain
punished). The method that he devises relieves him of
both fears. He need not use the whip, and the slaves'
hatred of him is diverted. Jack realizes that the slaves
have "no Affection to Act upon, but that of Fear, which
necessarily brought Hatred with it" (p. 143), but by
turning their fear into a semblance of gratitude, he can
control their hatred.

The contradictions in the master's comments point
to what he hides. He says he loves mercy, but he insists
that others do justice: he does not want to *see* it done
(pp. 130-131). Nevertheless, he is not squeamish about
imagining the violence he might inflict on others: ". . .

if I should come by, while they were using those Cruel-
ties on the poor Creatures, I should either sink down
at the Sight of it, or fly into a Rage, and kill the Fellow
that did it; tho' it is done too, by my own Authority"
(p. 145). This is not mercy, but fear, like Jack's, con-
cealed in outbursts of self-assertive rage.

Human relations, like most things in this book, are
frequently tainted by fraud. Jack's relationship to the
slave Mouchat is described in extravagantly emotional
terms, but it is based on two cruel hoaxes—that about
Mouchat's punishment, and an even crueler one to try
Mouchat's gratitude. Jack has a report spread that he
himself is to be hanged by the "Great Master" (p. 140).
After the grieving Mouchat finally offers to die for Jack
(p. 142), Jack reveals himself and extracts extravagant
semblances of affection from the slave (pp. 142-143). He
uses others as he uses the slave. As he inflicts various
injuries on his unfaithful wives, he pathetically longs
for public demonstrations of their affection. He seems
unaware of any emotional claims that might be made
on him, and he seems unconcerned about whether the
realities of others' feelings conform to appearances. The
public surface supersedes any private motives. He avoids
recognizing the fear and hatred that motivate the scen-
arios that he constructs.

The theological analogies to these human relationships are unsavory. The "Great Master," like a perverse
God, loves mercy but makes others do justice. Mouchat
offers himself to the "Great Master" as a substitute for
Jack in a crude version of atonement. The method that
Jack uses in dealing with the slaves is a confidence-game
version of salvation. The equivalent of the "Cruelest
Punishment" that the slaves are falsely threatened by
is a fraudulent hell designed only to "enhaunce the
Value of their Pardon" (p. 144). Jack himself experiences
a mild version of his method for exacting gratitude and

obedience from the slaves. He acknowledges the justice of God's taking everything from him, and is then grateful when God allows him to keep nearly all his fortune (pp. 170-171). It is unlikely that Defoe intended to blaspheme, but the base conception of human relations implied by this book provides no adequate analogies for a being not intended to be a sharper.

The narrator's allusions to the Bible display a mistaken arrogance verging on the comic. He is a John, although called Jack, and when he tells how people pitied him for not having parents, he alludes to the events associated with the birth of John the Baptist: "But I lay'd up all these things in my Heart" (p. 8). The reference is to Luke 1:66: "And all they that heard them laid them up in their hearts, saying, What manner of child shall this be! And the hand of the Lord was with him." Eventually Jack seems to be a version of Christ himself. When he and the Captain escape from a man who pursues them in the night, Jack says, "our Hour was not come, our Fate had Determin'd other things for us" (p. 91). In this sentence (in which he substitutes "Fate" for "Providence"), Jack alludes to the words that Christ spoke just before he was arrested: ". . . Sleep on now, and take your rest: it is enough, the hour is come; behold, the Son of man is betrayed into the hands of sinners" (Mark 14:41). Later, in dealing with the slaves, Jack plays the role of intercessor, a Christ figure. And repeatedly he refers to his tutor as a faithful steward and servant (pp. 125, 251), a reference to the "Lord's" commendation in the parable of the talents: "well done, thou good and faithful servant" (Matt. 25:21).

Jack's appropriation of these inappropriate biblical references raises the question of Defoe's relationship to the narrator. Clearly there is some irony at the expense of the young Jack, but perhaps we are to see him as developing, despite difficulties, into an essentially good

man, one who is, in the best sense of the word, a
gentleman. The question is this: does Defoe generally
recommend the narrator's view of the character he once
was, as in *Robinson Crusoe, Captain Singleton*, and *A
Journal of the Plague Year*, or is there an additional
irony at the expense of the narrator, as in *Moll
Flanders*?

The rumor that Defoe's prose tracts expound views
as dull-witted and contradictory as those of his most
uncomprehending narrators may deter some readers
from acknowledging what would otherwise seem to be
obvious ironies. But Defoe's treatise *The Compleat
English Gentleman* suggests the strong possibility of
extensive irony in *Colonel Jack*.[3] Of course anyone who
writes a long book about gentlemen arouses our suspicion of a possible perverted personal interest in the
subject. And Defoe does use a persona in his treatise,
apparently intending to publish it pseudonymously as
the work of one gentleman writing to another gentleman. One may well believe that Defoe was muddled
on the subject of gentility; nevertheless, he is not
muddled in the way that Colonel Jack is. The view of
gentility in *The Compleat English Gentleman* is not
the same as Colonel Jack's view, even after he matures.[4]

The theme of *The Compleat English Gentleman* is
the importance of education; an ignorant lout, even if
the son of a gentleman, has only the name of a gentleman. The writer insists that nature is depraved, and

[3] *The Compleat English Gentleman*, ed. Karl D. Bülbring (London: David Nutt, 1890). This was one of Defoe's last works, and
was not printed before Bülbring's transcription of the manuscript.

[4] For a differing point of view, see the following two studies, which
find little irony in the novel: William H. McBurney, "Colonel
Jacque: Defoe's Definition of the Complete Gentleman," *SEL* 2
(1962), 321-336; and Michael Shinagel, *Daniel Defoe and Middle
Class Gentility* (Cambridge, Mass.: Harvard University Press, 1968),
pp. 161-177.

that men unguided by instruction are "hurry'd down
the stream of their worst affections by the mere insensible impetuosity of nature" (*C. E. G.*, p. 111). "Gentleman" is not a fixed social position. The born gentleman
can lower himself, and one not born a gentleman can
become one. The writer sees wealthy tradesmen as a
group from which gentlemen are likely to arise; however,
the mere possession of wealth does not produce a gentleman. Indeed, it is unlikely that the man who makes
the wealth will ever achieve the requisite qualities:

> Purse-proud, insolent, without manners, and too
> often without sense, he discovers his mechanick
> quallificacions on all occasions; the dialect of the
> Alley hangs like a brogue upon his tongue, and if
> he is not clown clad in his behaviour, 'tis generally
> supplyed with the usuall air of a sharper and a bite,
> and he can no more leav the ravening after money,
> *Fas aut nefas*, than an old theif can leav off pilfer-
> ing, or an old whore leav off procuring (*C. E. G.*,
> p. 257).

The writer insists that he is not a "leveller" (*C. E.
G.*, pp. 19-31). He regards noble birth as a blessing, but
a blessing very easily lost. "Milk," he argues, is a more
powerful determinant than the parent's "blood"; how
many of noble blood have been suckled by commoners?
His rhetorical strategy here is to show that all blood
lines are corrupted (*C. E. G.*, pp. 75-79); he is probably
not primarily interested in arguing for the efficacy of
good milk. What the writer wishes to show is the
importance of having men with the qualifications for
performing the duties of gentlemen, regardless of their
bloodlines.

   A gentleman should, among other things, be patriotic.
The writer shows contempt for those who change sides
for personal reasons: "How often have these men of

honor, as *they are to be call'd*—for all gentlemen are or ought to be such—play'd Jack a both sides, to-day for and to-morrow against, to-day for the *Saxon* to-morrow for the *Swede*, as the money could be got or the party was the strongest" (*C. E. G.*, p. 30). A gentleman should neither be a mercenary nor let mercenaries take his place in battle (p. 64). In his family life, the complete gentleman is exemplary: "His conjugal life is all harmony and musick, peace and joy; tenderness and affeccion are the sum of their united enjoyment" (*C. E. G.*, p. 240).

Many of Colonel Jack's notions and actions are clearly in conflict with the conception of the gentleman in the later treatise. The narrator in *Colonel Jack* is much concerned to show his early natural superiority to those around him, despite his despicable education. Then and now, he accepts his father's dogma: ". . . the very hint would inspire me with Thoughts suitable to my Birth, and . . . I would certainly act like a Gentleman, if I believed myself to be so" (p. 3). The central theme of *The Compleat English Gentleman* is a contradiction of this notion. And of course the mere fact that Jack's well-born father and mother produced a bastard would, in the context of *The Compleat English Gentleman*, reflect adversely on their conception of gentility.

Not all that Jack does would be disapproved of in the treatise. His persistent attempts to gain an education are laudable, even if laughable. The complete gentleman must be liberally educated; however, a classical education, although valuable, is not essential. In his treatise, Defoe gives a favorable account of a man's education which resembles the account of Colonel Jack's. The man becomes a scholar through translations, but then also goes on to learn Latin (*C. E. G.* p. 207). Colonel Jack too reads much, and then goes on to learn some Latin from his tutor.

But Jack can hardly be called a scholar, and his subsequent career reflects the dubious success of his education. The military accounts that he reads send him on his ludicrous and ungentlemanly mercenary career in European wars. One must suspect that Defoe had Jack learn a little Latin not to establish him as a scholar but to suggest that Jack is interested in the externalities of learning rather than in essentials, a charge that Defoe makes against those who insist that only classical learning is of any importance (*C. E. G.*, pp. 200-201). Jack's whole career suggests his interest in simulations, rather than essences.

By the end of his story, Colonel Jack has put his family life into some order, and he has finally established his allegiance to King George. As a wealthy planter and merchant, he seems to be a likely candidate for gentility. But the warning in *The Compleat English Gentleman* against the residual effects of money grubbing is exemplified in *Colonel Jack*. Even while attempting to demonstrate his gentility on the battlefield, Jack is more interested in looting than in fighting. And Maximillan Novak shows that Defoe disapproved of such ventures as Colonel Jack's illegal trading with the merchants of Mexico, an incident occuring near the end of the book.[5] Jack is more aptly described as a greedy merchant than as a complete gentleman.

One must not be too harsh. To Defoe, Colonel Jack's achievements as a planter are considerable. And given his almost unspeakable education, much about Jack is commendable: "If he had come into the World with the Advantage of Education, and been well instructed how to improve the generous Principles he had in him, what a Man might he not have been" (preface). But

[5] *Economics and the Fiction of Daniel Defoe* (Berkeley and Los Angeles: University of California Press, 1962), pp. 122-127.

the obvious sympathy that is being shown for Jack should not be allowed entirely to obscure the plain sense of this statement in the preface. The narrator is a limited man whose greatness in only an unrealizable possibility.

The narrator's descriptions of his past continually betray the limits of his insight. He often comments mockingly on what he was, but he conveys his sense of the discrepancy between his past and his present more often than his sense of the discrepancy between his pretensions and his reality. His essential ironic perception might be paraphrased, "Isn't it amazing that *I* was ever like that?" Even from his final vantage, he sees no irony in his or his father's aspirations.

The opening sentence of the book shows that Jack has a relatively comfortable attitude toward his life: ". . . I am able now to look back upon it from a safer Distance, than is ordinarily the Fate of the Clan to which I once belong'd." His descriptions of his early crimes reveal a present complacency that obscures his sense of his past moral character. The fancied gentleman is conscious of his former raggedness: in describing his first venture as assistant to another pickpocket, he emphasizes his dress, particularly that he had no hat (p. 19). The now wealthy merchant is amused at his former poverty. When the money for this first venture is divided, he has no pocket to keep it in: "I have often thought since that, and with some Mirth too, how I had really more Wealth than I knew what to do with" (p. 22). In describing his first independent theft, he obviously identifies more closely with the wealthy merchant who is the victim than with himself, the thief: "This Careless way of Men putting their Pocket-books into a Coat-pocket, which is so easily Div'd into, by the least Boy that has been us'd to the Trade, can never be too much blam'd" (p. 45). This narrator has subdued the past that Singleton and Moll are so wary of. The "safer Distance" that he writes of is not only in time but in consciousness.

Jack's interpretation of his moral life is designed to give him ease. His early crimes, he says, are committed in a "State of Ignorance" (p. 40). Nevertheless, he also believes that his "uninstructed Conscience" prompts him to behave better than his companions (p. 55). The captain attributes Jack's self-preserving scruples to his being a "wary Politick Gentleman," but the narrator never accepts this explanation. All crimes that he cannot extenuate he excuses as the result of "necessity": "... It was a sad thing to be under a Necessity of doing Evil, to procure that subsistance, which I could not Support the want of" (p. 156). But Jack has earlier shown that even in the truly miserable circumstances of his childhood, he was capable of finding food and shelter honestly. He previously explained his crimes only as ignorance of the moral character of theft.

Although Defoe accepts "necessity" as an extenuation of crimes, those of his characters who use the conception of necessity for self-justification are nearly always attempting to deceive themselves or others. Colonel Jack's self-indulgent morality is exposed by contrast to that of his more scrupulous tutor. The tutor also states that he came into crime by necessity, but when Jack asks if he would not have to repeat his crimes if he were again in the same situation, the tutor replies "very sharply": "... I have some hope that I should venture to Starve, rather than to Steal; but I also beg to be deliver'd from the Danger, because I know not my own Strength" (p. 163). It is often difficult to distinguish Jack's morality from snobbery:

Now when I began to feel my self, as I may say, in the world; and to be arriv'd to an Independant

State, and to foresee, that I might be something
Considerable in time; I say, Now I found differing
Sentiments of things taking Place in my Mind; and
First, I had a solid principle of Justice and Honesty,
and a secret Horror at things pass'd, when I look'd
back upon my former life: That Original something,
I knew not what, that used formerly to Check me
in the first meannesses of my Youth, and us'd to
Dictate to me when I was but a Child, that I was
to be a Gentleman, continued to Operate upon me
Now, in a manner I cannot Describe . . . (p. 155).

Jack's repentance is the most perfunctory one in all
of Defoe's novels. Comfortably exiled in Mexico after
his second smuggling venture, he thinks over his life
and concludes that it was providentially ordered (p. 300).
He is aided in discerning the shape of his life by the
not entirely spiritual stimulus of "a violent Fit of the
Gout, which as it is allow'd by most People, clears the
Head, restores the Memory, and Qualifies us to make
the most, and just, and useful Remarks upon our own
Actions" (p. 307). He claims to learn *"To abhor myself
in Dust and ashes"* (p. 308), but his dust and ashes
are figurative; he is living in luxury, and finally rejoins
his wife in England "safe with all my Treasure" (p. 309).
Jack knows that money is essential; it separates him
from the ragamuffin that he once was. He also knows
that money is ultimately unsatisfying. Somehow the
making of money must be incorporated into the imaginary romance of his life. He persists in trading with
Mexico because he believes that he "had found the way
to have a Stream of the Golden Rivers of *Mexico* flow
into my Plantation of Virginia . . . I Dream'd of nothing
but Millions and Hundreds of Thousands" (pp. 296-297).
His dream is of a smuggler metamorphosed into a
conquistador: among the books he has read is "the

History of the *Spaniard's* Conquest of *Mexico*" (p. 157). And surprisingly enough, he does get to revel in the gold of his dreams. In Mexico, merchants turn goods into "Silver, or . . . Gold; so that their Warehouses, in a few Months, were piled up, even to the Ceiling, with Chests of Pieces of Eight, and with Bars of Silver" (p. 302). He is amazed at the bookkeeping operations that control such masses of wealth (pp. 302-303); the pen and ledger are mightier than the sword ever was.

Jack's stay in Mexico is the culminating experience in his search for gentility. Here Merchant Jack becomes in his own imagination Gentleman Jack. He lives the life of a noble Spaniard, something even better than being a colonel. The luxury and ceremony are all lovingly recounted (pp. 300-307). It is easy for him to repent of his former vulgar life; a Providence that brings him here is indeed beneficent. He does write of the difficulties of exile "in absence from my Family" (p. 309), but such pains are small in comparison with the pleasure he so obviously feels.

Strangely enough, the entire narrative preceding Jack's pleasant confinement and easy repentance manifests the same almost uncontrollable anxiety that one finds in Defoe's other books. In *Colonel Jack*, escape routes are obsessively listed in flurries suggesting breathlessness. On one occasion, street after street after street is listed; only "innumerable narrow passages, Alley's and Dark ways" (p. 20) escape enumeration. When Jack finally seems to have insulated himself from his past, having left no "gap open" (p. 263), his "tranquility" is destroyed by an "unseen Mine" (p. 264). These images define the situation of Defoe's characters. They must constantly imagine possibilities for disaster: anytime they fail to flee, someone or something will pursue.

In this novel too, the "law" is entangling and arbitrary. Jack's first wife and the tutor are, like Moll

Flanders, guilty of great evil, but they are severely punished for trifling or mistaken reasons. Justice can be done only through the most complicated of attitudinizing and reasoning.[6] The Spanish have laws that make it necessary for Jack to pay ransom to them, but make it impossible for them to collect it. The role playing, the fine reasoning, and the elaborate assuming that lead to the foreknown conclusion are all described (pp. 280-284). The bizarre legality of the Spaniards is an example of the legal subversion of the laws that fascinates Defoe. Legal entanglements are the most honest of human relations in this book; an honest man insists on drawing up documents that will protect others from him (p. 125).

The almost inexplicable confidence of the narrator is not derived from his dubious repentance: "... how far it pleases God to give the Grace of Repentance where he gives the Opportunity of it, is not for me to say of myself" (p. 309). He firmly believes in his metaphor—gentleman. The book has shown the tawdriness of the conception, but Jack does not doubt its efficacy. The metaphors of Defoe's other characters disintegrate, leaving dissatisfaction and anxiety, but this time Defoe has chosen to sustain his narrator's ignorant assurance. That truncated repentance can have only one function: to provide at least a frail support for Jack's misplaced faith. He can blithely enjoy his gentility in the belief that he has done the decent thing by religion.

This easeful ending is in part prepared for by the resolution of the psychosexual conflicts. The shadow of Oedipus, as lengthened by Freud, is on this book. Although one hesitates to claim that Defoe understood the Freudian interpretation of the Oedipus myth, *Colo-*

[6] George A. Starr, *Defoe and Casuistry* (Princeton: Princeton University Press, 1965), discusses the background of this aspect of Defoe's writings.

nel Jack does evidence an intelligible concern with the relations of fathers, mothers, and sons.[7]

Jack's father abandons him, leaving the boy only the injunction to be a gentleman like his father. Jack tries desperately and with little success, especially in matters of love and war. But finally he asserts himself against the man who has debauched one of his wives: ". . . can'd him as severely as I was able . . . till he roar'd like a Boy soundly whipt" (p. 243). This man has refused a duel, and Jack now reverses the humiliation resulting from his own former refusal to duel. He has now asserted himself in the physical way that his father, the colonel, might have approved. But he not only emulates the father; he also supplants him. Jack separates a grown man from his sexual partner, and reduces him to the condition of a boy.

The Oedipal suggestions that are abundant in this entire episode are emphasized when Defoe has Colonel Jack recount a version of the myth to explain his wife's intemperance:

> That was a good Story, whether real or invented, of the Devil tempting a young Man to murder his Father. No, *he said*, that was un-natural. Why, then *says the Devil*, Go and lye with your Mother: No, *says he*, That is abominable. Well, Then, *says the Devil*, If you will do nothing else to oblige me, go and get Drunk; Ay, ay, *says the Fellow*, I'll do that, so he went and made himself Drunk as a Swine; and when he was Drunk, he murdered his Father, and lay with his Mother (p. 241).

This reduction of high tragedy to a temperance lesson does not quite disguise the connection between violence to fathers and desire for mothers.

[7] James Walton, "The Romance of Gentility," *Literary Monographs* 4 (Madison: University of Wisconsin Press, 1971), pp. 98-110, analyzes this aspect of *Colonel Jack* persuasively and in detail.

Jack repeatedly supplants fathers. He insists on marrying Moggy without her father's consent; he is her father's "master" (p. 247). In Virginia, he takes his first wife back only after his tutor wishes to marry her. The tutor is one of many permutations of the father throughout the book.[8] Jack's "Master" in Virginia "sat in a Seat like a Lord Judge upon the Bench, or a Petty King upon his Throne" (p. 122). Jack first comes before him like a "Malefactor," but eventually Jack too becomes a wealthy planter with arbitrary powers. Finally Jack submits and makes his peace with a father figure— King George.

In the final episodes, those exertions that were so difficult for him are no longer necessary. His wife manages his peace with the king, and his confinement among the merchants of Mexico is a succession of passive pleasures. He achieves that self-centered self-confidence that he displays in writing his memoirs.

Colonel Jack is a variation of the picaresque novel. Its materials are picaresque, but its hero is not. The opening is the traditional account of the hero's scandalous birth, but it is delivered without the usual contemptuous tone (p. 3). Jack goes on to live the picaro's life, one demanding a hard-boiled concern for survival, but he does not learn the picaro's lessons. Although his experiences reveal gross realities, he continues to cherish those dreams whose falsehood his life exposes. He is not, however, quixotic. He reacts as basely as anyone else, yet never ceases to believe in what his actions deny. Defoe is exploring those psychological aspects of the

[8] Starr, *Defoe and Casuistry*, p. 98, briefly discusses father figures in the book. He comments on Jack's relationship to his parents: "If he matures, it is never, in my opinion, to the point of treating others on terms of equality; he is forever the aggrieved orphan, showing either what a splendid son he would have made if his parents had not abandoned him, or what a splendid parent he would have made if he had been in their situation" (p. 98).

picaresque that are normally suppressed. The picaro's relation to his absent family is ordinarily not resolved but eliminated as an inessential concern in a hard world. But it is precisely the concern for his absent family that makes Jack cling tenaciously to his airy notions of gentility.

Issues, characters, and motifs are often repeated in Defoe's works, but the repetition is rarely identical. Defoe tries to understand by writing; and as he repeats, he clarifies and develops. Colonel Jack's character is adumbrated in *Memoirs of a Cavalier*, published in 1720, four years before *Colonel Jack*. Much of the earlier book is more closely allied to history than to fiction, but the somewhat intermittently presented central character is nevertheless extensively developed. The wars that he fights in are among those on which Colonel Jack's imagination is nurtured, the campaigns of Gustavus Adolphus and the English Civil War (see *Colonel Jack*, pp. 10-11, 157).

This cavalier is legitimate. Although the book suggests a loose definition of "gentleman"—a clever servant who acquires some money is treated as one (*M. C.*, pp. 65-68)—its hero's credentials are impeccable.[9] He is the son of a gentleman with a substantial estate. The portents that precede his birth are described without the barest suggestion of irony (*M. C.*, p. 7). He receives an excellent education (*M. C.*, pp. 9-10): ". . . a Gentleman ought always to see something of the world . . ." (*M. C.*, p.10).

Despite this promising beginning, the cavalier has the limitations of youth and inexperience. He has a series of tricks played on him in France (*M. C.*, pp. 12-14); through his impetuosity, he mistakenly kills a man (*M. C.*, pp. 17-18); and he runs away while observing his

[9] *Memoirs of a Cavalier*, ed. James T. Boulton (London: Oxford University Press, 1972). All subsequent references are to this edition.

first battle (*M. C.*, p. 24). He blushes for mistaking a
courtesan for a lady (M. C., pp. 32-33), but he nevertheless suggests that he received his sexual initiation despite
pangs of conscience (*M. C.*, p. 34). He is much like
Colonel Jack, except in one important respect—the
cavalier commits these errors at an appropriate age.

His military career too has a superficial resemblance
to Jack's, but the cavalier develops in competence and
temperament in ways that Jack does not. The cavalier
becomes a soldier out of vanity rather than commitment
to a cause, and he is soon praised for valor that he
himself knows is only indiscretion (*M. C.*, p. 76). But
when civil war breaks out in England, his character
takes a more serious turn. He has earlier seen the
brutalities of war (*M. C.*, pp. 44-45), and after the out-
break of fighting in England he blames himself for the
previous "Unconcernedness of my temper at the approaching Ruin of my native Country" (*M. C.*, p. 125).
He is troubled about the bitter realities of war for which
Jack's concern for his skin and gentility give him no
leisure.

The cavalier's war experiences are not exclusively
heroic. His woundings are quite inglorious (*M. C.*, pp.
176, 183); he misses a battle while visiting some ladies
(*M. C.*, p. 189); and he and his fellow soldiers once
disguise themselves as plowmen with a woman, an
episode that ends in a most unmilitary battle with some
country louts (*M. C.*, pp. 209-210). In all this, however,
the cavalier is not shown as an unusually foolish man;
he merely lives in a world where such things happen.

The cavalier has the ties to family, king, and country
which bring him into inner conflict. He finally finds a
providential order in all of the "Confusions," noting the
errors that both his side and Parliament have committed
(*M. C.*, pp. 270-279). Colonel Jack's version of gentility
is trivial in comparison; he imitates the least conse-

quential aspects of a gentleman's life. He does not recognize, as the cavalier does, that a gentleman shares the difficult life of others, that he differs from others because his duties are greater.

Memoirs of a Cavalier shows that Defoe saw an alternative to Jack's notions of gentility: his creation of the colonel is deliberate. The two books are almost romance and anti-romance. But only almost. *Memoirs of a Cavalier* is not quite romance, and *Colonel Jack* is not entirely in opposition to it. Defoe displays such obvious pleasure in describing the rituals of gentility that one must suspect him of sharing his narrator's interests. But however attractive Jack's irresponsible simulation of the life of a gentleman may be, Defoe is not confined to his character's limits. He understands those uncomfortable anomalies that Jack has suppressed.

Defoe is less insistent than usual on the moral purpose of *Colonel Jack*. Near the end of the book, the narrator states that while writing he did not foresee the popularity of autobiographical stories such as his, implying that such popularity imposes a moral obligation to include more instruction than he has included. He seems almost embarrassed at the limitations of his commentary, rather casually hoping that the reader "will reap the benefit of my Misfortunes, perhaps, more than I have done myself" (p. 307). In the preface, however, the "editor" makes the usual claim that the story is justified by its moral. Despite the contradiction, preface and story suggest the same thing: Defoe is on the verge of acknowledging that he writes fiction. In this preface, he abandons one of the former justifications of his stories—literal truth: ". . . neither is it of the least Moment to enquire whether the Colonel hath told his own Story true or not; If he has made it a *History* or a *Parable*, it will be equally useful, and capable of doing Good" (preface). Defoe suggests in other prefaces that details have been changed and events disguised or allegorized, but not that they may be merely illustrative.

Defoe expends unusually little effort on finding consistent nonliterary justifications for *Colonel Jack*, and a great deal on the literary surfaces of the work. Although it shows the usual narrative carelessness, *Colonel Jack* has a carefully wrought verbal surface—one capable of scaffolding the metaphysical abysses that open almost inadvertently in Defoe's other works. George Starr comments on the "prose style rich in figures of balance"; "worldly and otherworldly values alike are affirmed: *Colonel Jack* comprehends both, but without ultimately ranking or reconciling them."[10]

Out of his usual motifs and themes, Defoe has created an unusual, and somewhat incongruous, final equilibrium. *Robinson Crusoe* is concluded by the exhaustion of its central figure, not by a resolution of his conflicts. Captain Singleton's repentance seems to be fraud: it merely disguises Singleton's painfully achieved, although sordid, identity. Moll Flanders arrives at a tenuous equilibrium by interpreting and transforming her past; however, Defoe suggests the suppressions and distortions that are needed if she is to maintain her stability. In the *Journal*, H. F. repents, but only a small, although intense, segment of his experience has been explored. He is somewhat different from the other characters in that he need not reorder an entire lifetime. Colonel Jack's repentance is perfunctory, but he achieves the equanimity that Crusoe, Singleton, and Moll lack. With assurance he incorporates his past into his repentant future. Defoe shows the failures of Jack's life to us, but he gives no indication that Jack, like Moll,

[10] Starr, *Defoe and Casuistry*, pp. 83, 84.

is suppressing his past only with difficulty. Colonel Jack is the most self-possessed of Defoe's narrators. His confidence in the magical words that conceal appalling truths is left unshaken.

VII

Roxana: The Verbal World

Defoe's last novel, commonly called *Roxana*, was published in 1724 under the title *The Fortunate Mistress: or, a History of the Life and Vast Variety of Fortunes of Mademoiselle de Beleau, afterwards called the Countess de Wintelsheim in Germany Being the Person known by the Name of the Lady Roxana in the time of Charles II.*[1] As the title suggests, the world of this novel glitters more, and more falsely, than that of any other of Defoe's novels. The same palliations of a despiritualized world as those offered in the other novels are here brilliantly displayed but vehemently discredited: money is inefficacious, sexuality perverse, and emotions murderous. The moral evasions of Defoe's other heroes are judged in Roxana. Even the legerdemain of repentance fails, and Roxana's past persistently asserts itself. At no point can she look back on a life safely and satisfyingly ordered. A dead husband reappears; a not entirely welcome former lover turns up on her doorstep; and a disagreeable daughter cannot be bought off. Roxana enters her pursuing daughter's presence even while trying to evade her: "... I was to conceal myself, if possible, and yet had not the least room to do any-thing towards it; *in short*, there was no retreat, no shifting any-thing off; no avoiding or preventing her having a full sight of me ..." (p. 278).

[1] References are to *Roxana*, ed. Jane Jack (London: Oxford University Press, 1964).

In this last novel, evil is obscurely but persistently present. The midwife provided by the prince "look'd ... like one set privately to dispatch me out of the World" (p. 77). Amy believes that Roxana's first husband would "in any convenient Place ... have murther'd her" (p. 87). The raging Jew of Paris, a "devilish Fellow," lays "a hellish Snare" for Roxana (p. 136); but when he threatens to expose the prince, he is caned and mutiliated (pp. 133-134). People in this book commit violence, even murder, to conceal themselves.

That the guilty perceive others' guilt most readily is a recurrent conception in Defoe's works: "Where deep Intrigues are close and shy/ The Guilty are the first that spy" (p. 67). Roxana knows that her fears of murder are not idle. Her hatred of her daughter Susan and her maid Amy's murder of the girl are the final and compelling testimonies to Roxana's identification with the malevolent world that she sees. The violence outside is also within. Susan is not only a daughter; it is also Roxana's given name.

In Defoe's novels, a common metaphor for depravity is the loss of sensation: "stupid" and "senceless, deaf" are the words that Roxana uses to describe herself (p. 159). She feels "profound tranquility" in her liaison with the prince, but this feeling is only evidence that "Lethargick Fumes doz'd the Soul" (p. 69). For Roxana, to be fully sentient is to experience pain. She assumes that all pleasurable feelings are superficial and conceal a grimmer truth. Pleasure is less real than pain, and her ability to feel painful emotions is evidence that she is not entirely depraved.

Roxana's moral judgments on herself give her an identity. As her roles change, she ascribes an unchanging inner world to herself. However, experience teaches her not of the reality of an inner moral world but of the reality of appearances. Adultery, she once says, is a matter of contiguity and memory: "... if the Man and the Woman part, there is an End of the Crime, and an End of the Clamour; Time wears out the Memory of it or a Woman may remove but a few Streets, and she soon out-lives it ..." (p. 153). According to the Dutch merchant, acknowledging a bastard removes the "Infamy" if no one, including the child, knows anything to the contrary (pp. 227-228). The honest Quaker remains honest only because she continues to appear so to herself as well as to others:

> My dear Friend, the Quaker, was kind, and yet honest, and wou'd do any-thing that was just and upright, to serve me, but nothing wicked, or dishonourable; that she might be able to say boldly to the Creature, if she came, she did not know where I was gone, she desir'd I wou'd not let her know ... (p. 302).

Only Roxana's painful self-judgments and her imaginings of disaster convince her that within her many appearances is a differing single identity. Her feelings of guilt validate her belief in a spiritual dimension to her being.

Roxana's morality is a counterpoise to her experiences. She constructs an opposition between feeling and principle. Her first experience of love is with her landlord, not her husband: "... I began ... to love him too, and that in a Manner that I had not been acquainted with myself" (p. 35). But her judgment has nothing of love in it: "... I receiv'd his Kindness at the dear Expense of Body and Soul, mortgaging Faith, Religion, Conscience, and Modesty, for (as I may call it) a Morsel of Bread ..." (p. 38). His comforting bread and affection remain in opposition to her scathing abstractions. To retain an inner identity differing from her behavior, she must define her actions in contemptible terms and judge them harshly. For example, during her liaison with the prince, she describes with pleasure her beauty and the prince's relish of it (p. 73), but then reduces all to a matter of her "carcass" and his "blindness" (pp. 74-75). And one motive for Roxana's putting Amy to bed with the landlord is that this action defines her pleasing relationship to the man as unequivocal wickedness: ". . . this is enough to convince any-body that I did not think him my Husband, and that I had cast off all Principle, and all Modesty, and had effectually stifled Conscience" (p. 46). In deliberately releasing these sexual impulses in herself, the landlord, and Amy, and then subsequently defining her relationship to the landlord by means of the most aberrant episode in it, Roxana prevents herself from feeling any moral confusion. After his death, she gives us the prim reminder that she never called him "husband" (p. 55). In this way, she maintains her equilibrium in a self-created inner world that contrasts with her actions.

Roxana repeatedly comments on the numbing effect of the stifling of conscience, but she does not in fact suffer this presumed effect: ". . . Conscience left off speaking where it found it cou'd not be heard" (p. 44; see also p. 69). Defoe's other novels have, like *Roxana*, a retrospective point of view: the narrator comments on his former self. But the moral and narrative patterns differ in *Roxana*. In the other novels, the central characters lose their sense of their moral condition as they harden, and they recover it only during repentance: most of the moral commentary is inserted from the perspective of the social security that comes with money and old age. With some exceptions, Roxana remains generally conscious of her evil choices. She sins knowingly, although unrepentantly, at the end of her career as well as at the beginning. Much of her moral commentary is written from the point of view of her final

undefined debacle, but she also makes many of her harsh
reflections on her conduct during the period of her
sinning. Her guilt asserts itself strongly during her "Life
fill'd with all humane Felicity" (p. 264). A lifetime of
insisting on her evil gives her an overwhelming consciousness of it; she creates a conscience, and it will
not be subservient to her.

Roxana's vigorous assertions of moral principles keep
her conscious of a world purer than the one that she
lives in, but her morality is undiscriminating and impossible of application. It distorts her feelings rather than
governs them. When she meets her implacable daughter,
Roxana finds it "a secret inconceivable Pleasure ... to
know that I kiss'd my own Child; my own Flesh and
Blood, born of my Body.... But I rous'd up my Judgment and shook it off" (p. 277). Judgment, which is
traditionally associated with morality, has here the
function of keeping Roxana from acting according to
either her morality or her feelings.

During the early part of her liaison with the prince,
Roxana relaxes her moral point of view. Nearly all the
moral strictures at the beginning of this episode are from
a later point of view. She at first abandons herself to
the pleasures of glittering surfaces without insisting on
the counterview of conscience. Her description of her
fortnight with the prince suggests no response to anything other than to a social surface: ".... for to have
the entire Possession of one of the most accomplish'd
Princes in the World, and of the politest, best bred Man,
to converse with him all Day, and, *as he profess'd*,
charm him all Night; what could be more inexpressibly
pleasing ..." (p. 68). She insists on no other dimension;
all is external. His gifts become the substance of love.
They are sexually exciting: "... behold, I saw my Neck
clasp'd with a fine Necklace of Diamonds ... If I had
an Ounce of Blood in me, that did not fly up into my

Face, Neck, and Breasts, it must be from some Interruption in the Vessels; I was all on fire with the Sight ..."
(p. 73). Roxana and this man are unconnected to the moral and social worlds that exist independently of them. Nothing transcends their relationship to each other: "... as the Prince was the only Deity I worshipp'd, so I was really his Idol ..." (p. 70). In one bizarre episode, Roxana proves to herself as well as to the prince that she is an unadulterated surface, a monument to the integrity of the superficial. She proves that she wears no cosmetics: "... I put a Handkerchief into his Hand, and taking his Hand into mine, I made him wipe my Face so hard, that he was unwilling to do it, for fear of hurting me" (p. 72).

Roxana's retrospective comments on her life are scathing: "... the dirty History of my Actings upon the Stage of Life ..." (p. 75). But at the time of her relationship with the prince, she temporarily accepted herself—the sum of her behavior—without creating an interior voice to comment. She feels exhilarated rather than debased. Near the end of her liaison, however, she must wonder what she will be without him—his gifts, his conversation, his desires. Will something of her survive his departure? She finds her continuity in the moral being that she then resurrects. She again articulates a view contradictory to her behavior and desires. She preaches repentance to him, but "I was a Hypocrite; for had I prevail'd with him really to be honest, I had lost him, which I could not bear the Thoughts of" (p. 108).

In her next sexual relationship, that with the Dutch merchant, she presents feminist arguments against marriage (pp. 147-159). She is protesting against the loss of identity which she associates with her former submission to the prince: "... the very Nature of the Marriage-

Contract was, in short, nothing but giving up Liberty,
Estate, Authority, and every-thing, to the Man, and
the Woman was indeed, a meer Woman ever after, that
is to say, a Slave" (p. 148); ". . . the Pretence of Affection,
takes from a Woman every thing that can be call'd
herself; she is to have no Interest; no Aim; no View;
but all is the Interest, Aim, and View of the Husband
. . ." (p. 149). Roxana resists the notion that she is no
essential thing but only the creation of her circumstances. Nevertheless, even her argument against submission seems to be the product of momentary exigencies. She admits that her feminist arguments are a
pretense; she merely wants to control her money, a
motive "too gross . . . to acknowledge" (p. 147). Nevertheless, she is moved by her own arguments; in the midst
of her powerful description of a woman's plight, she
remarks, "He did not know how feelingly I spoke this"
(p. 150). However, in the interstices of her passionate
exposition, she still insists that her view is unnatural.
Despite her protestations to the contrary, it *is* her view:
". . . I had a mortal Aversion to marrying him, or indeed,
any-body else . . ." (p. 161). Her contradictions here, as
elsewhere, serve her needs: her feminist argument satisfies the demands of a precariously ordered ego, and
rejecting the same argument gives her a sense of continuing to participate in a morally stable world.

The surfaces of Roxana's life are stubbornly autonomous and fragmented. She uses costume not only for
utilitarian purposes—disguise and hypocrisy—but also to
create a new, although temporary, self. While she dances
in her Turkish costume, the name "Roxana" is fixed
upon her "as effectually as if I had been Christen'd"
(p. 176). The description of this costume is lavish beyond
what is customary in Defoe, and its origin—its ancestry
—is explained:

... in less than half an Hour I return'd, dress'd
in the Habit of *a Turkish Princess*; the Habit I
got at *Leghorn*, when my *Foreign Prince* bought
me a *Turkish* Slave, as I have said, the *Malthese*
Man of War had, it seems, taken a *Turkish* Vessel
going from *Constantinople* to *Alexandria*, in which
were some Ladies bound for *Grand Cairo* in *Egypt*;
and as the Ladies were made Slaves, so their fine
Cloaths were thus expos'd; and with this *Turkish*
Slave, I bought the rich Cloaths too ... (pp. 173-
174).

Later Roxana wears the costume for her husband, and
she repeatedly thinks of the pleasure of her first appearance in it. Even when her daughter's knowledge of the
incident is a danger, Roxana "cannot help confessing
what a Reserve of pride still was left in me; and tho'
I dreaded the Sequel of the Story, yet when she talk'd
how handsome and how fine a Lady this Roxana was,
I cou'd not help being pleas'd and tickl'd with it ..."
(p. 287). The costume creates a self not entirely subordinated to either moral or prudential considerations.

Roxana later adopts the Quaker costume for disguise,
although she is not, like Moll, in legal difficulties or,
at this time, in a position to lose something by scandal.
Her wish is to "transform" herself "into a new shape"
(p. 209). She wishes to abandon the shape of Roxana,
created by a dancing dress. The Quaker costume, like
the Turkish one, has its own identity before Roxana
acquires it: she insists on buying one of her landlady's
old suits. Although her expressed motive is to hide, she
achieves more. She becomes indistinguishable from
what she imitates: "... I dress'd myself in the Dress
I bought of her, *and said*, Come, I'll be a Quaker to-Day,
and you and I'll go Abroad; which we did, and there

was not a *Quaker* in the Town look'd less like a Coun-
terfeit than I did . . ." (p. 213).

In the powerful final episode, Roxana's daughter
Susan pursues her through the multiplicity of disguises:
"*. . . like a Hound* she had had a hot Scent . . ." (p.
317). Susan is implacable. The worldly methods of
Roxana and Amy do not affect her. She will not be
deterred by bribes, by pleadings that she consider her
self-interest. By the venal standards to which Roxana
is accustomed, Susan is not civilized. She allows no
changes of role, no obscuring of what is real. Roxana's
many changes cause her to fear being Proteus without
a shape of her own; but now Susan defines her as a
mother. What has previously been altogether too easy
for Roxana—the shifting of identities—has become impossible.

Susan is all the abandoned children in Defoe's novels.
They have been ignored or bought off, and now they
claim their relationship. There is nothing discreet that
Roxana can do. But she adamantly refuses to acknowledge the relationship, despite the failure of all her
attempted evasions. Amy then exercises the only alternative to disclosure—she kills Susan. Roxana cannot
deny her obvious responsibility.

Susan wants nothing of Roxana but to be acknowledged. "She is my Mother; and she does not own me,"
the girl cries in a scene that brings tears to the eyes
of even her antagonist the Quaker (p. 304). Susan is
convinced, erroneously, that her mother is too "tender
and compassionate" to "let her perish" (p. 308). Although she knows much that is damaging to Roxana,
she makes no attempt to use the information against
her. She is implacable about nothing but her desire for
a mother.

Why then does Roxana feel that she is "brought to

the Point of Destruction" by the girl (p. 296)? The possible effects of scandal do not justify the rage, despair, and near madness of both Roxana and Amy (for example, pp. 272-273). Roxana's most comprehensive explanation of her responses again suggests her need for detachment from others, the same need exhibited in her feminist arguments: "... I must for-ever after have been this Girl's Vassal, *that is to say*, have let her into the Secret, and trusted to her keeping it too, or have been exposed, and undone; *the very Thought fill'd me with Horror*" (p. 280). Roxana's mode of attaining psychic equilibrium is to condemn her wickedness internally, not publicly. To acknowledge this daughter is to acknowledge her past, to make it public, to fix it. Admitting her evil only to herself, while changing public identities, is her way both of retaining a sense of inner coherence and of partially denying the reality of her actions. If the knowledge of her evil is shared by someone outside her, it becomes external fact, not a manipulable inner defense. Susan's pathetic intransigence destroys Roxana's carefully constructed life.

Children link Roxana, like Moll, to her past. What distresses Roxana is that they are connected to her without simply being extensions of her. Mutely or vociferously, they assert their claims and make their judgments. They appeal to feelings that Roxana cannot easily stifle. She wants them at a distance, emotionally and physically. When they grow up, she thinks of bringing them back into her life, but only if she can manage to put a "new Face" on it:

> I had begun a little, *as I have said above*, to reflect upon my Manner of Living, and to think of putting a new Face upon it; and nothing mov'd me to it more, than the Consideration of my having three Children, who were now grown up; and yet, that

> while I was in that Station of Life, I cou'd not
> converse with them, or make myself known to them;
> and this gave me a great-deal of Uneasiness ... (p.
> 207).

She wants them to return only when she is prepared
to deceive them about the past.

She identifies with her children, especially in sexual
matters. She cannot bear the thought that her daughter
might "be drawn in to lie with some of that course cursed
Kind, and be with-Child, and be utterly ruin'd that way"
(p. 197). And she chooses a wife for one of her sons,
"a beautiful young Lady, well-bred, an exceeding good-
natur'd pleasant Creature" (pp. 263-264). She cannot,
however, bear any resistance from her children. When
her son at first rejects the girl she has chosen for him,
she is angered and remains spiteful even after the
subsequent marriage. The prince's affection for their
bastard child is "one great Tye to him, for he was
extremely fond of it" (p. 82); Roxana, however, rejects
such ties. She chooses the more manageable jewels,
costumes, and money. The life that she creates out of
the opposition of her private judgments and her attractive public surface is stable, if sterile. This carefully
calculated life is threatened by the messy appeals of
children.

Amy is the only person who is allowed in Roxana's
life without reservation. But she is only nominally an
other. Although she acts by herself, she acts only from
Roxana's motives: Roxana's description of her is,
"faithful to me, as the Skin to my Back" (p. 25). When
terrified in the storm, Roxana thinks to herself: *"Poor
Amy! What art thou, that I am not? What has thou
been, that I have not been?* Nay I am guilty of my
own Sin, and thine too ... as we had sinn'd together,
now we were likely to sink together" (p. 126). As mothers

too, they are one. Roxana agrees to take Amy's daughter by the landlord as her own: "... had not I a hand in the Frolick..." (p. 48). Later, Amy is Roxana's emissary to her abandoned family:

> Amy made quite another Figure than she did before: for she went in my Coach ... and there was indeed, no real Difficulty to make Amy look like a Lady, for she was a very handsome well-shap'd Woman, and genteel enough; the Coachman and Servants were particularly order'd to show her the same Respect as they wou'd to me (p. 194).

The guilt for Susan's murder is Roxana's because Amy acts as Roxana's surrogate—but not only for that reason. Amy's rage is shared by Roxana: Roxana says of Susan, "had she died by any ordinary distemper, I should have shed but very few Tears for her" (p. 302). Although Roxana turns against Amy in the closing section, Amy speaks Roxana's desires:

> *Amy* was so provok'd, that she told me, *in short*, she began to think it wou'd be absolutely necessary to murther her ... and I, *says I in a Rage*, as well as I love you, wou'd be the first that shou'd put the Halter about your Neck, and see you hang'd, with more Satisfaction than ever I saw you in my Life; nay, *says I*, you wou'd not live to be hang'd, *I believe*, I shou'd cut your Throat with my own Hand; I am almost ready to do it, *said I*, as 'tis, for your but naming the thing; with that, I call'd her cursed Devil, and bade her get out of the Room (pp. 270-271).

Roxana's relish in imagining Amy's death is an outlet for the rage that she does not want to contemplate—that against her daughter.

Roxana states that all Amy's schemes were "the Effect of her Excess of Affection and Fidelity to me" (p. 271). Yet Amy has even less rational cause to be enraged at Susan than Roxana does. Why should she go beyond what Roxana authorizes and murder the girl? After the murder, Roxana says, "to have fall'n upon *Amy*, had been to have murther'd myself" (p. 302). Why does Roxana feel that she dare do nothing to punish Amy? Exposing Amy will give Roxana no legal responsibility for the murder. And if Roxana is merely metaphorically equating scandal with suicide, she is making nonsense of all the guilt that she is describing. Roxana persistently attempts to explain everything according to the categories of common-sense rationalism (while inwardly indulging in guilt-ridden fantasies of supernaturalism), but her explanations of her and Amy's behavior in the concluding segments of the book are even less plausible than they were earlier. The relationship of Amy to Roxana goes beyond ordinary categories of common interests, legal responsibilities, or normal affections.

Roxana's putting Amy to bed with the landlord is her way of enjoying Amy: ". . . I sat her down, pull'd off her Stockings and Shoes, and all her Cloaths, Piece by Piece, and led her to the Bed to him . . . I fairly strip'd her, and then I threw open the Bed, and thrust her in" (p. 46); "I stood-by all the while" (p. 47). This action is repeated until Amy is pregnant (p. 48). The earlier conversations of Amy and Roxana are often about sexual matters. Even before the landlord has indicated any sexual interest, Amy argues that Roxana should respond to his advances. When Roxana is recalcitrant, Amy offers to take her place: "Why look you, Madam, if he would but give you enough to live easie upon, he should lye with me for it with all my Heart. That's a Token, *Amy*, of inimitable Kindness to me,

said I, and I know how to value it; but there's more
Friendship than Honesty in it, *Amy*" (p. 28). Roxana
explains Amy's later enticement of the landlord: ". . .
the Girl lov'd me to an Excess, hardly to be describ'd
. . ." (p. 31). After the landlord has given them provisions,
Amy, who sleeps with Roxana, gets up "two or three
times in the Night, and danc'd about the Room in her
Shift; in short, the Girl was half distracted with the
Joy of it; a Testimony still of her violent Affection for
her Mistress, in which no Servant ever went beyond
her" (p. 32). Roxana notices, or thinks she does, that
the landlord has no hesitation in performing sexually
in Amy's presence: ". . . We had both of us us'd *Amy*
with so much Intimacy, and trusted her with every
thing, having such unexampled Instances of her Fidelity, that he made no Scruple to kiss me, and say all
these things to me before her, nor had he car'd one
Farthing if I would have let him Lay with me, to have
had *Amy* there too all Night" (p. 36). And Amy volun-
teers, "I must put you to-Bed to night together" (p.
36). Both participate by imagination in every aspect of
the other's sexuality.

Amy's sexual behavior remains a matter of intense
interest to Roxana. The threesome of landlord, Amy,
and Roxana is recalled repeatedly (pp. 84, 130) and
almost reduplicated with Roxana's "Man of Honour"
(p. 187). Also Amy's relationship with the prince's servant—"*like* Mistress, *like* Maid" as Amy puts it (p.
83)—is alluded to repeatedly (pp. 83, 86, 131, 216). Amy's
sexuality is a matter of such importance to Roxana that
it figures in asides having little to do with the narrative:
". . . at last I employ'd my Maid *Amy*, such I must be
allow'd to call her, (notwithstanding what has been said
of her) because she was in the Place of a Maid-Servant;
I say, I employ'd my Maid *Amy* to go to him . . ." (p.
111).

Roxana's corruption of Amy is the archetypal sin of
the book. She destroys Amy's autonomy, making Amy
one with her morally and sexually: "... I cannot say
but that it was something design'd in my thoughts, that
my Maid should be a Whore too..." (p. 47). From that
point on, Amy is another version of her mistress. Roxana's subsequent career is devoted to a strict separation
of outer and inner: those who exist autonomously cannot share her inner world, and the one who shares it
must lose her separate identity.[2]

The early sexual sin and the final sin—the murder
of Susan—are related. Amy has become Roxana's "only
Relief" (p. 265), and one of her functions is to keep
children away. Amy has a motive for the murder: Susan
threatens to supplant her. If Susan is acknowledged,
the special relationship of Amy to Roxana will be ended.
Amy and Susan are opposites: one representing the
interests of a narcissistic world, the other, the demands
of a larger responsibility.

The Quaker is the only person other than Amy who
is allowed glimpses of Roxana's private world. Roxana
withholds the details of her past on the principle *"that
Secrets shou'd never be open'd without evident Utility"*
(p. 326); nevertheless, she is willing to trust her with
sordid details. When Susan seems to to be piecing
together Roxana's past, Roxana thinks of her Quaker
friend: "... I cou'd more freely have trusted her, than
I cou'd the Girl, by a great-deal; *nay*, I shou'd have
been perfectly easie in her" (p. 284).

Roxana knows that the Quaker is needy, and she
corrupts her by her gifts: "... for by this I engag'd her

[2] See Homer O. Brown, "The Displaced Self in the Novels of Daniel
Defoe," *ELH* 38 (1971), 582: "The witness is the dangerous other.
Roxana, by watching Amy's seduction by the same man who has
ruined her, has rendered Amy safe. She has made her an accomplice,
an adjunct to her own will."

so, that as I found her a Woman of Understanding, and of Honesty too, I might, upon any Occasion, have a Confidence in her ..." (p. 213). Roxana's language is staid, but what she wants is a woman who will not make use of, or be too shocked by, the lurid facts that she may acquire. Roxana chooses her friend well. She soon learns that "*Quakers* may, and that this Quaker did, understand Good-Manners, as well as any-other people" (p. 285). What Roxana means is that the Quaker takes an interest in her amorous concerns. She takes pains to bring Roxana and the Dutch merchant together in her house; with Amy, she puts them to bed after the marriage; and she visits the couple before they arise the next morning (pp. 244-245). She has an adequately lascivious imagination, being able quickly to grasp the sexual implications of Susan's restrained account of Roxana's past (p. 287). The Quaker William was a bourgeois pirate; this Quaker is a bourgeois bawd. When, after the marriage, Roxana rewards her with a large sum of money, she almost faints, but recovers in a perverse confusion of money, love, and pain: "... she flew to me, and throwing her Arms about my Neck, O! *says she, thou has almost kill'd me*; and there she hung, laying her Head in my Neck for half a quarter of an Hour, not able to speak, but sobbing like a Child that had been whipp'd" (p. 253).

Roxana wishes to substitute the Quaker for Amy in order to escape the oppressive sense of accumulated evil that is associated with Amy. The Quaker's appearance of gravity, her refusal to lie outrightly, her unwillingness to see evil—all give her the appearance of moral health. Nevertheless, she, like Amy, is a creature made in Roxana's image. Roxana calls herself and the Quaker widows (p. 254), a somewhat evasive formulation (the Quaker has been deserted). Roxana's feeling of sympathy for the Quaker arises from her remembrance of her

own similarly straitened past. The symbiotic relationship of the two is emphasized by costume. Roxana
assumes the Quaker's costume; but when she once
appears in her old Turkish costume ("not a decent Dress
in this Country"), the Quaker "*merrily said*, that if such
a Dress shou'd come to be worn here ... she shou'd
be tempted not to dress in the *Quakers Way* any-more"
(p. 247). She ends up acting "in Amy's stead" (p. 326).

The murder of Susan is the final rejection of any
external claim. The abrasive but stabilizing relationship
between Roxana's inner and outer worlds collapses, and
she is at the mercy of her dreams and fantasies:

> ... she haunted my Imagination, if she did not
> haunt the House; my Fancy show'd her in a
> hundred Shapes and Postures; sleeping or waking,
> she was with me: Sometimes I thought I saw her
> with her Throat cut; sometimes with her Head cut,
> and her Brains knock'd-out; other-times hang'd up
> upon a beam; another time drown'd in the Great
> Pond at *Camberwell*... (p. 325).

No longer can Roxana convince herself of her moral
nature by condemning herself extravagantly (what
comment on the murder will be extravagant?). Her inner
reality becomes her only one: she is wicked. Even before the murder, that inner world was asserting itself
strongly, bringing her to the point of madness:

> ... I grew sad, heavy, pensive, and melancholly;
> slept little, and eat little; dream'd continually of
> the most frightful and terrible things imaginable:
> Nothing but Apparitions of Devils and Monsters;
> falling into Gulphs, and off from steep and high
> Precipices, *and the like*; so that in the Morning,
> when I shou'd rise, and be refresh'd with the Bless-
> ing of Rest, I was *Hag-ridden* with Frights, and
> terrible things, form'd meerly in the Imagination;

and was either tir'd, and wanted Sleep, or overrun
with Vapours, and not fit for conversing with my
Family, or any-one else (p. 264).

Her prosperous exterior is inefficacious—it no longer
counterbalances her judgments of herself—and the subsequent murder of Susan irrevocably delivers her to her
monstrous fantasies. Her world is internal, and she is
unable to control it. For Roxana, the external world
has been reduced to a metaphor for her evil.

Roxana's final misfortunes are unspecified; they are
the "Blast of Heaven" (p. 330). This metaphoric storm
is the powerful culmination of many related images.
Storms (especially at sea), darkness, and tides are prominent in the narration both literally and symbolically.
These images are conventional metaphors of the religious consciousness, but in *Roxana* they become subtle
revelations of the narrator's mind.

The storm in which Roxana and Amy are caught while
traveling by sea from France to Holland is described
at length. In traditional fashion, Roxana interprets it
as a providential warning, having as its purpose the
awakening of conscience.[3] However, she remains
unrepentant although terrified, and subsequently
storms become for her a symbol of God's impending
judgments. In addition, storms become a personal, not
entirely traditional, symbol. Just before the storm
begins, Roxana "secretly wish'd that a Storm wou'd rise,
that might drive the Ship over to the Coast of England"
(p. 122). She has just had an accession of patriotic fervor
at seeing "Beloved *England* ... which I counted my
Native Country, being the Place that I was bred up
in, tho' not born there" (p. 122). She was born in France,

[3] George A. Starr, *Defoe and Spiritual Autobiography* (Princeton:
Princeton University Press, 1965), p. 166, points out that the
experience that Amy and Roxana undergo at sea is one often
described in spiritual autobiography.

has traveled in Italy, and is now on her way to Holland.
Patriotism becomes a momentary refuge for her belea-
guered identity. But instead of bringing her an identity,
the storm threatens to destroy her, body and soul. It
represents not only God's vengeance but especially a
general physical disintegration:

> ... *Death in any Shape has some Terror in it*; but
> in the frightful Figure of a Storm at Sea, and a
> sinking Ship, it comes with a double, a trebble, and
> indeed, an inexpressible Horrour, and if I were that
> Saint you think me to be, which, God knows, I am
> not, 'tis still very dismal; I desire to die in a Calm,
> if I can ... (p. 137).

Storms represent Roxana's often nearly unbearable
sense of inner conflict. The channel storm is itself
internal as well as external; it follows upon her wishes,
and causes her to look on her life with "Contempt and
Abhorrence" (p. 127). But she has only a "silent sullen
kind of grief" with "no Sence of Repentance" (p. 129).
Less literal uses of the image often do not indicate a
moral judgment: the storm is for Roxana anything that
is a source of stress. The prince's reformation, although commendable, is a "Storm upon" her (p. 107).
The pursuit by Susan too is a storm: "it look'd more
threatening every Day" (p. 281); "the Clouds began to
thicken about me" (p. 296).

Roxana feels that she is caught in inexorable and
terrifying currents. Of her relationship with the prince,
she comments, "But the highest Tide has its Ebb; and
in all things of this Kind, there is a Reflux which
sometimes also is more impetuously violent than the
first Aggression" (p. 107). She uses a metaphor of the
sea to explain the satisfaction that she takes in her
accumulating wealth, but the metaphor also suggests
drowning: "... I went on smooth and pleasant; I wal-

low'd in Wealth, and it flow'd in upon me . . ." (p. 188).
She stabilizes herself as always by balancing pleasure
against pain, inner judgment against external appearance. But the internal and external are increasingly and
inextricably confused in her mind. Storms, seas, currents, and tides are internalized, and the threat is within
as well as without. Pleasure itself is a destructive force:
". . . the Tide of Pleasure continues to flow . . . till
something dark and dreadful brings us to ourselves
again" (p. 69). She associates pleasure with the sea and
with the loss of identity, and the "dark and dreadful"
with self-definition. In either case, there is no refuge
for her.

Images of sea, storms, and darkness are a metaphoric
base for the narrator's language even when she is making
no overt judgment about herself. After her first husband's desertion, "the Terrors behind me look'd blacker
than the Terrors before me . . ." (p. 43). When speaking
of woman's difficulties in marriage, she says that "in
her Husband, she sinks or swims, as he is either Fool
or wise Man; unhappy or prosperous; and in the middle
of what she thinks is her Happiness and Prosperity, she
is ingulph'd in Misery and Beggary . . ." (p. 149). The
Dutch merchant's proposal of marriage, as well as Roxana's rejection of it, is presented in hackneyed nautical
terms: ". . . that we wou'd be upon one Bottom, and
I shou'd steer: Ay, *says I*, you'll allow me to steer, *that
is*, hold the Helm, but you'll conn the Ship, *as they
call it*; that is, as at Sea, a boy serves to stand at the
Helm, but he that gives him the orders, is Pilot" (pp.
150-151). After their separation, the image becomes one
of terror:

> . . . when after the Shipwreck of Virtue, Honour,
> and Principle, and sailing at the utmost Risque in
> the stormy Seas of Crime, and abominable Levity,

I had a safe Harbour presented, and no Heart to
cast-Anchor in it. His Predictions terrify'd me . . .
and fill'd my Head with a thousand Anxieties and
Thoughts, how it shou'd be possible for me, who
had now such a Fortune, to sink again into Misery
(p. 162).

Later, in her relief at her marriage to the merchant
she is

like a Passenger coming back from the *Indies*, who
having, after many Years Fatigues and Hurry in
Business, gotten a good Estate, with innumerable
Difficulties and Hazards, is arriv'd safe at *London*
with all his Effects, and has the Pleasure of saying,
he shall never venture upon the Seas any-more (p.
243).

These images are a way of thinking, and eventually the
terror associated with their symbolism invades every
aspect of her life.

Roxana's terror is intermittently opposed by the
romance world that she creates.[4] The materials of that
world are the remembered affluence and religion of her
early years. Her parents were wealthy Protestant refu-
gees from France. She is not orphaned early, only
married imprudently. She differs from the picaresque
hero in nearly every respect but the essential one—she
is compelled to shape her own identity. Her life develops
in a way far removed from her childhood circumstances,
and she sees her romance world, her virtue and affluence, as fraudulent. Her childhood provides an ideal
against which she judges her later simulations. Only

[4] James Walton, "The Romance of Gentility," *Literary Monographs* 4 (Madison: University of Wisconsin Press, 1971), pp. 122-
135, discusses perceptively and in detail the function of "romance"
in *Roxana*.

intermittently does she feel that she is a plausible continuation of the child that she was; her persisting sense of herself is that she is an imposter. Romance and reality for Roxana are, respectively, virtue and vice.

Roxana uses wealth and religion metaphorically to create her idealized world. She describes her ready acceptance of the prince as a response commensurate with religious dedication: "... no Virtue was Proof against him, except such, as was able too, to suffer Martyrdom ... so much goodness, join'd with so much Greatness, would have conquer'd a Saint ..." (p. 65). His gifts of jewels and costumes are described lovingly. The undescribed climax of her "romance" is her liaison with the king: "... three years of the most glorious Retreat, *as I call it.* .." (p. 182). The formula *"as I call it"* directs attention to Roxana's metaphoric use of *"Retreat."* The word had in Defoe's time a moral connotation—a time of contemplation—although not necessarily a specific religious significance. Roxana's retirement with the Quaker too is a "Retreat" (p. 211). The term is less obviously misapplied when used to describe her time with the Quaker than when used to describe her liaison with the king, but for that reason it is even more hypocritical. The word conceals evil more efficiently when it is less openly metaphoric.

Roxana combines her sense of both romance and reality in her frequent ironic uses of the word "honor." For example, her child by the prince is "my little *Son of Honour*, as I call'd him" (p. 96), and her later perverted lover is "a Person of Honour" (p. 183). Both as actor and narrator, she is aware of the irony, commenting later, "how foolish and absurd did it look, to repeat the Word Honour on so vile an Occasion" (p. 201). Nevertheless, the irony is not simple, and the word pleases her. Her contemptuous treatment of gallants does not diminish her intense interest in the genteel world. The

Dutch merchant's suit is finally successful because of the titles he offers. And on their meeting in London, he overcomes her resentment by speaking the language of courtly love, an assimilation of religion to chivalry: "... he had done a long, and (he hop'd) a sufficient Pennance for the Slight that I had suppos'd he had put upon me ..." (p. 226); "... I wou'd find some Reasons to forget his first Resentments, and to think that Pennance, *as he call'd it*, which he had undergone in search of me, an *Amende Honorable*, in Reparation of the Affront given to the Kindness of my Letter of Invitation, and that we might at last make ourselves some Satisfaction on both sides, for the Mortification past" (p. 227).

Roxana's world becomes increasingly immaterial. Mind comes to have a greater weight than the physical reality proposed by common sense: "oppressed with the Weight of my own Thoughts" is Roxana's description of her condition (p. 53). Her world is crowded with things, and for a time her reality is metaphoric—an equation of mind and matter, a tension of external and internal. But gradually the surrounding world loses its validity for her. She calls herself a "mere *Malade Imaginaire*," who "may as easily die with Grief, or run-mad with Joy ... as if all was real" (pp. 238-239). She grasps at words; she is enamored of the "Name of *Princess*" (p. 235), and resolves to be both lady and countess (p. 242). Her final calamity is that she is abandoned to her subjective consciousness.

Roxana is susceptible to language and uncomprehendingly preoccupied with it. Her language is rich in metaphors, sometimes pungent ones; for example, marrying a man after yielding to him sexually "is to befoul one's-self and live always with the Smell of it" (p. 152). She frequently calls attention to her metaphoric language by some variant of the formula "as I called it."

She defines herself verbally, and her preoccupation with language is related to her concern for her identity. She refuses to go to a priest, although she desires the comfort of a confession; unable to explain why she should now "scruple any thing," she merely concludes, "'tho I was a Whore, yet I was a Protestant Whore" (p. 69). She is bilingual—French and English—and later learns Italian and Dutch. Not knowing the language of a country is to her a frightening experience; to some degree, she loses her sense of her own reality. Her fears in the channel storm are increased by her not understanding the sailors, "neither when they curs'd, or when they pray'd" (p. 123). When she next sets out for Holland, she takes someone along who understands Dutch, and she soon learns the language herself. She sometimes implies that language is of enormous importance; yet at the same time, she evokes a shadowy, ambiguous world beyond it. She says, for example, that the Quaker "had as much apparent Sincerity, and I verily believe as real, as was possible to be express'd" (p. 251). This statement suggests that "expression" is both a limited and the only measure of reality.

The major satiric works bracketing the most flourishing period of satire in the eighteenth century are *A Tale of a Tub* (1704) and the fourth book of *The Dunciad* (1742). Both provide a perspective on the condition that Defoe reveals in *Roxana*. In *A Tale of a Tub*, Swift describes an attempted disjunction of the external from the internal world. The *Tale* illustrates two complementary processes: first, the metaphoric externalization and trivialization of the spiritual; and second, the withdrawal into the despiritualized inner world of imagination and, finally, madness. The clothes philosophers turn the soul into a suit; the Aeolists turn the spirit into wind; and the narrator turns man's will into vapors. The external world is regarded as a mechanism, and is consequently trivial: "How shrunk is every Thing, as it appears in the Glass of Nature? So, that if it were not for the Assistance of Artificial *Mediums*, false lights, refracted Angles, Varnish and Tinsel; there would be a mighty Level in the Felicity and Enjoyments of Mortal Men" (Section IX). The narrator recommends flight from this depressing world into fiction, imagination, and madness.

In *The Dunciad*, Pope more abstractly and generally analyzes the condition that Swift describes in the *Tale*. The goddess Dulness urges man to reduce nature to a dimension narrow enough to conceal its coherence:

> O! would the Sons of Men once think their Eyes
> And Reason giv'n them but to study *Flies*!
> See Nature in some partial narrow shape,
> And let the Author of the Whole escape. . . .
> (IV, 11. 453-456)

The "gloomy Clerk" then defines the result of the goddess's recommendation:

> Make God Man's Image, Man the final Cause,
> Find Virtue local, all Relation scorn,
> See all in *Self*, and but for self be born. . . .
> (IV, 11. 478-480)

Language should be the mediator between the internal and external worlds; it should connect the external world of nature to the internal one of spirit, revealing the divine order of the whole. But the Dunces have eliminated the referential function of language: "Since Man from beast by Words is known,/ Words are Man's province, Words we teach alone" (IV, 11. 149-150). When man no longer uses words to define or create the coherence of a larger world, his words become things in themselves, and he is in danger of becoming a prisoner in a self-created verbal jail. Swift and Pope define the solipsism that Roxana creates and suffers from. She is finally punished by being imprisoned in the private world from which she has eliminated all but her monstrous self. Defoe shows this private world to us, and we see her as pitiable, not arrogant like the Dunces.

In *Robinson Crusoe*, language is a barrier—a limit and a defense; language cannot communicate the most intense feelings, but neither does it allow the aberrations of human emotion to go unchecked. *Roxana* becomes an expression of the central figure's internal state. Language no longer protects Roxana from the forces within. To a degree, it organizes the inner world by articulating it, but it provides no barriers. Roxana is at the mercy of the fantasies that she describes.

Roxana is Defoe's most extreme expression of the isolation, the diminishing sense of external reality, that is experienced by all his characters. From Crusoe to Roxana, they fear their disintegration in the flux of life. They grasp at anything, trying to create their identities by accretion. But as they appropriate the external world to themselves, it loses its specificity. They sense that they are seeing only their own reflections. At this point, Defoe's characters usually repent and attempt to reassemble themselves according to some normal pattern. They reassert their faith in an unseen providence, in a visible material world, and in themselves. This faith becomes more difficult to achieve, and the sequence of novels ends in Roxana's inability to repent. Although Colonel Jack's perfunctory repentance goes unchallenged by Defoe, Jack seems often to be living in an imaginary world that is conjured up by his language: the patterns of his life (the three Jacks, his series of wives, his imitations of gentility) are precariously balanced between internal and external. Roxana's world is finally reduced to the network of words that she uses to define her inner turmoil.

In novel after novel, Defoe comes back to the same problems, exposing the same nerves again and again. There are no solutions in *Roxana*, only fewer evasions. One suspects that the nightmarish sense of isolation that he creates in the ending of *Roxana* is to some degree the reflection of his own feelings. These feelings of isolation are perhaps part of the cause of the voyeurism that persists and increases in his novels. Voyeurism is hinted at in Moll's early fantasies of the older brother as she lies in Robin's arms; in *Colonel Jack*, there is actual threesome sex with one woman looking on; and in *Roxana*, the voyeurism becomes a prominent part of the plot. The intensity absent from the viewer's own experience is sought in the experience of others.

It is probable that to some degree Defoe recognized his personal implication in the scenes that he created. The relationship of tales to their tellers is so often commented on by Defoe's characters that it is unlikely that Defoe had not also considered his own relationship to his tales. One of the most persistent needs of his characters is to tell their stories, often with necessary alterations and omissions. Roxana comments of good news that she hears about her children, "You may believe I heard this with the same pleasure which I feel now at the relating it again" (p. 25). The Puritan justification for fiction—the edification of others—is subverted if the author recognizes his personal gratifications from writing. If writing is self-expression, the created world of *Roxana* is only with difficulty reconciled to a moral purpose. It is not surprising that Defoe wrote no more novels.

In the preface to *Roxana*, Defoe accepts more responsibility for his writing than he does in any other preface. He continues to insist that he is working from a factual document, part of which he can vouch for, but he takes full responsibility for the literary art: any failures "the

Relator says ... must be from the Defect of his Performance; dressing up the Story in worse Cloaths than
the Lady, whose Words he speaks, prepar'd it for the
world" (p. 1). Also, he gives the central figure full credit
for censuring herself (p. 2); it is primarily the relating
that he takes responsibility for, not, as in *Moll Flanders*,
primarily the morality. The ironic perspective in *Roxana* is clearer and more consistent than in any other
novel by Defoe. The central figure's precise understanding of many of her failures allows little play for the
kind of moral muddle one finds so abundantly in *Robinson Crusoe*, in *Captain Singleton* and, to a lesser degree,
in *Moll Flanders*. Nevertheless, this irony implicates
the author in his novel. The clarity brought about by
the author's ironic distance from his subject leads to
his perceiving the unresolvable contradictions of his own
creation.

Defoe changed in the short time between the publica-
tion of "An Essay on Honesty" in the *Serious Reflections of Robinson Crusoe* and the writing of *Roxana*.
In the *Serious Reflections*, he writes, "No man is so
hardened in crimes as to commit them for the mere
pleasure of the fact—there is always some vice gratified;
ambition, pride, or avarice makes rich men knaves, and
necessity the poor" (p. 34).[5] But Moll Flanders cannot
explain why she continues to steal; and Roxana's reiterated question "What was I a Whore for now" (pp.
201-203) remains unanswered. Roxana's stock motive—
money—is finally not plausible even to herself. The
vehemence with which she defines her relationship with
the "Person of Honour" as whoredom betrays her fear
that even so unmistakable a relationship might confuse
her: "... he then turn'd his Discourse to the Subject

[5] References are to *Serious Reflections during the Life and Surprising Adventures of Robinson Crusoe*, ed. George Aitken (London:
J. M. Dent, 1895).

of Love; a Point so ridiculous to me, without the main thing, I mean the Money, that I had no Patience to hear him make so long a Story of it" (p. 183). Although Moll and Roxana eventually abandon their crimes, they can find no satisfactory explanations of their former motives. And Roxana cannot repent even when she sees the course of her life clearly.

The moral world of the *Serious Reflections* is less complicated than that of the novels, especially *Roxana*. In "An Essay on Honesty," Defoe deals with the "necessity" that his characters invoke so often. He has great sympathy for those who have been forced to violate the usual moral codes because of physical distress. Repeatedly he expresses and implies his belief that one's judgments on other men should be tempered by a consideration of the provocations that they may have suffered. He suggests that the honesty of a prosperous man is of little moral significance; a poor man in debtor's prison may be as honest as his rich creditor (*S. R.*, p. 34). Nevertheless, in cases of transgression of God's expressed commandments, "necessity" provides no moral excuse (Defoe does excuse cases of unavoidable ignorance); Defoe's point is that God "has bid us not despise the thief that steals in such a case; not that the man is less a thief, or the facts less dishonest" (p. 35). Clearly Defoe believes that every man has some point at which he will be unable to resist temptation; he cites Satan's accusation against Job as probable: ". . . strip him a little . . . and you will quickly see your good man be like other men" (*S. R.*, p. 39). Defoe notes, however, that Satan was mistaken about Job.

Although even an ordinarily good man may on occasion fail, man's moral duty is not abrogated in even the greatest distress. Five starving men at sea eat one of their number in order to survive: ". . . at best 'twas doing evil that good may come, which is expressly forbidden" (p. 36). If a man is starving and steals bread, the moral question is not about the cause of the stealing but about the fact of ownership: "If it be his, and not my own, I cannot do it without a manifest contempt of God's law, and breaking the eighth article of it, 'Thou shall not steal.' Thus as to God, the crime is evident, let the necessity be what it will" (*S. R.*, p. 42). When Roxana bitterly condemns herself for committing adultery, she has, according to Defoe's moral scheme, a strong claim on our sympathy but, nevertheless, a correct view of her actions.[6] Even if she is acting to preserve her life, "a Woman ought rather to die, than to prostitute her Virtue and Honour" (p. 29). All Defoe's characters who use "necessity" to exculpate themselves are self-deceived. However, necessitous circumstances do, and are intended to, secure the reader's sympathy. As George Starr shows, Defoe often causes the reader to respond sympathetically to things that he might normally judge harshly.[7] Such a separation of judgment and sympathy is consonant with Defoe's views as expressed in "An Essay on Honesty," but it also leads to complicated moral tangles in the novels.

[6] See Maximillian Novak, *Defoe and the Nature of Man* (New York: Oxford University Press, 1963), pp. 65-88, for a different interpretation of *Roxana* and the problem of "necessity" in Defoe's fiction: "It would be a mistake ... to confuse Roxana's tortured self-condemnations with a final judgment on her life, since, unlike Jack or Moll, she narrates her story during the anguish and remorse of Christian repentance" (p. 87). According to my reading, Defoe's view is that one's sympathy for a person does not alter the moral nature of his actions. Defoe might very possibly have consigned a character to damnation while sympathizing with his plight.

[7] *Defoe and Casuistry* (Princeton: Princeton University press, 1971): "Nearly all of Defoe's fictional works cause us to identify imaginatively with characters whose actions we regard as blameworthy. At the same time that they compel sympathy, his heroes and heroines evoke moral judgment, and our two responses are often sharply opposed" (Preface, p. v).

What Defoe has not fully recognized in "An Essay on Honesty" comes increasingly to the fore in his novels: psychological needs, seemingly unrelated to survival, may be just as coercive as more easily recognized "necessities." Roxana tries to explain her necessity as "bread" when it is a related but far more complicated need. The landlord has already given her food, and has promised that "he would no more oppress my Gratitude now, than he would my necessity before" (p. 34). What she now needs is emotional security, kindly jesting, and frivolity, as well as joints of meat and glasses of wine. What he offers her is irresistible but unassimilable into any moral scheme available to her: ". . . I sinn'd, knowing it to be a Sin, but having no Power to resist . . ." (p. 4). She cannot will the absence of the kindness that she condemns.

During her liaison with the prince, Roxana attempts to incorporate her perception of her psychological necessities into a moral scheme: ". . . I satisfy'd myself with the surprizing Occasion, that, as it was all irresistable, so it was all lawful; for that Heaven would not suffer us to be punish'd for that which it was not possible to avoid . . ." (p. 69). She means that all was irresistible because of the attractiveness of the prince, not because of any need for survival. She accepts the formulation temporarily but, in retrospect, calls her reasoning "these absurdities" (p. 69).

In "An Essay on Honesty," Defoe considers cases of material necessity, especially matters of food and money. But once the possibility of psychological necessity is admitted, Defoe's and Roxana's neatly delineated traditional moral world is obscured. Moral judgments become confused and confusing assessments of characters' inner worlds. In novel after novel, Defoe shows men and women engaged in obsessive behavior that is rationalized but not explained. Even the characters themselves often sense their loss of self-control. Roxana loses control of her life although seeming in Defoe's terms to understand the moral implications of her behavior. She knowingly persists in evil while finding it repulsive. Defoe's creation of Roxana implies his recognition of psychological necessities, even if he calls them absurdities. He has Moll Flanders reorganize her life according to her somewhat slipshod morality, but he grants no such reorganization to Roxana, a far more perceptive character. The precise moral world of "An Essay on Honesty" is blurred by Roxana's perceptions and needs.

The book's ending is consistent with its heroine's development and with the development of Defoe's fiction: ". . . my Repentance seem'd to be only the consequence of my Misery, as my *Misery* was of my Crime" (p. 330). This final statement implies Roxana's belief in a moral order that punishes crime with misery; however, her despising a miserable condition is not evidence of repentance. She is imprisoned within herself and can see only her evil. In a similar predicament, Moll Flanders finds at least temporary assurance of the validity of her repentance through a lengthy process of introspection. When reunited to Jemy, she finds that her earlier feelings are revived; she then believes in the possibility of recovering an earlier moral state. Although Roxana sees herself as monstrous, she can find no steps to retrace. The fictions that Defoe's other characters use to reconstruct their lives are unconvincing to her. Their moral systems provide a structure for them only because they see themselves less clearly than Roxana sees herself. Having created a character who reveals the limitations of his own and his previous characters' moral assumptions, Defoe could only stop writing novels—or write a new kind. Sin and repentance, the conceptions that he had used to order his works, gradually diverged from their traditional religious meanings. It is possible that Defoe had originally planned to have Roxana repent, but it also seems reasonable to assume that the book is finished. Defoe stopped when he reached the end.

Index

Alemán, Mateo, 50

Baine, Rodney M., 110-111n
Bastian, F., 109, 121
Benjamin, Edwin B., 42n
Berne, Eric, 43
Booth, Wayne, 14n
Boyce, Benjamin, 25n
Brooks, Douglas, 75n
Brown, Homer O., 5n, 169n
Bunyan, John: *Grace Abounding*, 51-52, 107-108; *Life and Death of Mr. Badman*, 52; *Pilgrim's Progress*, 51, 124

Columbus, Robert R., 77n

Damrosch, Leopold, Jr., 14n
Defoe, Daniel: *Captain Singleton*, 48-74, 75, 76-77, 104, 126, 139, 182; *Colonel Jack*, 17, 49, 125, 126-154, 180, 181; *Compleat English Gentleman*, 139-141, 142; *Conjugal Lewdness*, 80-85, 106; *Due Preparations For the Plague*, 108; *Journal of the Plague Year*, 107-125, 126, 139; *Jure Divino*, 6; *King of Pirates*, 54-55; *Memoirs of a Cavalier*, 150-152; *Moll Flanders*, 17, 49, 74, 75-106, 125, 126, 127, 139, 181, 182, 186; *Review*, 6; *Robinson Crusoe*, 6, 17, 20-47, 49, 51, 53, 54, 60, 62n, 74, 75, 104, 126, 139, 180, 182; *Robinson Crusoe, Serious Reflections of*, 21-22, 30, 34, 182-185; *Roxana*, 6, 17, 19, 127, 155-187; *Shortest Way with the Dissenters*, 14-16; *True-Born Englishman*, 16

Ellis, Frank, 31
Erickson, Robert A., 3

Fielding, Henry, 108

Gay, John, 70
Gildon, Charles, 20-21

Halewood, William H., 29n
Henry, Matthew, 120
Hume, David, 11-12
Hunter, J. Paul, ix-x, 18n, 42n, 109n, 119n

James, E. Anthony, 14n
Johnson, Samuel, 45-46

Kerby-Miller, Charles, 3
Kernan, Alvin, 47
Krier, William, 75n
Kumar, Shiv K., 61

Landa, Louis, 108n
Lazarillo de Tormes, 56-57
Locke, John, 6-9, 11, 12

McBurney, William H., 139n
MacLean, Kenneth, 6n
McMaster, Juliet, 77n
Memoirs of Martinus Scriblerus,
   3-4, 9-11
Miller, Perry, 116n
Miller, Stuart, 48-49, 51n
Moore, John Robert, ix, 66n

Novak, Maximillian, x, 2, 6, 17n,
   70n, 75n, 127n, 142, 184n

Parker, Alexander A., 50
Paulson, Ronald, x
Pope, Alexander, 1, 2, 47; *Dun-
   ciad,* 2-3, 179-180

Quevedo y Villegas, Francisco
   Gómez de, 50

Richardson, Samuel, 52, 107-108

Rogers, Pat, x

Schonhorn, Manuel, 62n, 109n
Schrock, Thomas S., 46n
Scrimgeour, Gary, 71
Secord, Arthur, 48, 57n
Shinagel, Michael, 139n
Smollett, Tobias, 50
Spectator, 7-8
Starr, George A., x, 18n, 42n, 89n,
   109n, 112n, 113n, 123n, 147n,
   149n, 153, 172n, 184
Sutherland, James, ix, 13, 66n
Swift, Jonathan, 1, 2; *Modest
   Proposal,* 3, 16; *Tale of a Tub,*
   44, 46-47, 178-179

Walton, James, 92-93n, 148n,
   175n
Watt, Ian, x, 29n, 75n
Wolff, Cynthia Griffin, 18n